# DOWN TO EARTH

# JAMAICAN COOKING

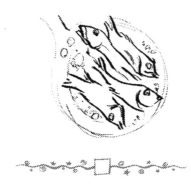

# DOWN TO EARTH

## JAMAICAN COOKING

BY

## LAURICE
## DE GALE

Sister Vision
Black Women and Women of Colour Press

96 97 98 99 ML 5 4 3 2 1


**Canadian Cataloguing in Publication Data**
DeGale, Laurice
Down to Earth Jamaican Cooking
Includes index
ISBN 1-896705-00-6
1. Cookery, Jamaican. I. Title
TX716.J27D44 1996   641.597292   C95-932923-4


Edited by Margaret Adam
Book Design, illustrations and layout: ARTWORK
Editor for the Press: Makeda Silvera
Production: Stephanie Martin


Represented in Canada by the Literary Press Group
Distributed in Canada by General Distribution
Represented and distributed in the U.S.A. by InBook
Represented in Britain by Turnaround Distribution

Printed in Canada by union labour


**SISTER VISION**
**Black Women and Women of Colour Press**
P.O. Box 217, Station E
Toronto, Ontario
Canada  M6H 4E2
(416) 595-5033

*This book is dedicated to Philipp.*

*Without your love, support*

*and encouragement*

*this would not have happened.*

# TABLE OF CONTENTS

INTRODUCTION

**7**
APPETIZERS & SNACKS

**21**
SOUPS

**31**
MEAT, POULTRY & GAME

**57**
SEAFOOD

**79**
EASY ON THE BUDGET BUT NUTRITIOUS

**87**
VEGETABLES, LEGUMES & SALADS

**120**
ROOTS, FOOD & TING

**127**
PASTRIES & CAKES

**140**
PORRIDGES

**144**
FRUITS FOR DESSERTS

**149**
DRINKS & BEVERAGES

**163**
GLOSSARY
COOKING HINTS
INDEX

# INTRODUCTION

Why write a book on Jamaican cooking? So many of my friends have coaxed and encouraged me to do so over the years, that I finally decided . . . why not? As an immigrant to Canada, traditional Jamaican cooking was my only tie to the lush, tropical culture I had left behind. Sitting down to a spicy aromatic dish of Curried Goat with Rice and Peas or Ackee and Saltfish was the perfect antidote to the cold weather and strangeness of my newly chosen home. As one of over 400,000 Jamaicans living in Canada, I have shared my culture with friends from many ethnic backgrounds. Over the years I threw many dinner parties and functions, introducing friends from various backgrounds to the rich, pungent flavours of Jamaican cuisine. Often, guests would ask me for the recipes to certain dishes and I would laughingly tell them there were none. My cooking style, much like my mother's, was 90% pure instinct.. A little of this, a little of that, a taste to adjust the flavours. . . . that was my method of cooking.

The decisive moment came in March 1993, when a friend approached me, looking quite forlorn. She confided to me that her husband, a Jamaican by birth, had brought home five Snappers, and asked her to prepare them for him. Unfortunately, my friend had no idea where to begin and asked me to write out a recipe for her. She didn't know what a challenge that would be for me!

I had never written down a recipe, or even considered recording one on paper. My mother would have laughed at my dilemma. My sisters and I learned to cook by example, from our mother — much the way she herself had learned. My mother's meals were always exceptional and perfectly seasoned. In her days, writing down a recipe would have been considered to be

1

something of a disgrace. Instead, recipes were passed down from mother to daughter, their passage relying solely upon memory and the talent of each apprentice. Putting together a recipe for my Brown-Stewed Snapper took a concerted effort, calculating and translating instincts into actual measurements. My efforts were rewarded, when my friend, pleased as a punch, proudly announced that the recipe had been a hit with her husband!

Following that experience, and recalling numerous similar situations with friends and acquaintances, I decided it was time. I would write a cookbook sharing a few of the great secrets of Jamaican cooking. It would be a mouth-watering collection of the down-to-earth recipes my mother had taught me as a young girl.

My first step in preparing this book was to return to Jamaica to visit my mother. As my teacher and mentor, I wanted her expert judgment and finally, her seal of approval on my recipes. With everything she had taught me, this cookbook could not be completed without her input. Sure enough, she laughed when she heard I was going to write a cookbook. And while she considered it a "no-no," she was proud to share, through me, the unique contributions Jamaican cooking has made to international cuisine.

My mother has always been a wonderful cook and a great economist. Widowed at a young age, with ten children to feed, she created miracles in the kitchen on an extremely tight budget. Her skill at improvising delicious, practical and nutritious meals formed the basis for my own cooking style and the title of this book.

As children, my mother taught only the girls to cook. My brothers were excluded, as in those days, men were not tolerated in the kitchen. By the age of fifteen, my sisters and I were each capable of preparing a meal for eleven. Since then, times have changed and my brothers have also learned to cook. My brother Oliver's savory recipe for Mannish Water (page 26) is proof that it's never too late to learn!

Our meals were made from a wide selection of foods. Fresh pork, beef and fish were purchased at the market, while we reared goats, poultry and rabbits on the farm for our own consumption. Callaloo, okra, cabbage,

tomatoes, legumes, yams, cocos, and sweet potatoes were grown in our back-yard. Tropical fruits such as mangoes, papayas, soursop, otaheite apples, guavas, the citruses — to name a few — were always in abundance. At that time refrigerators were uncommon, therefore fresh foods, especially meat and fish, were bought in small quantities and consumed quickly.

Weekends were a special time for meals. Saturdays, my mother would make a rich Beef Soup for dinner. The soup was a delicious concoction of beef, dumplings, thyme and escallion, overflowing with hearty chunks of pumpkin, yams, cocos, carrots and turnips. The definitive touch was the addition of an unbroken Scotch Bonnet pepper, which simmered along with the rest of the ingredients, gave a delectable, peppery flavour to each mouth-ful.

Fricassee Chicken was our all-time Sunday favourite, served with steaming rice and peas and a fresh green salad. With meals we drank fresh squeezed carrot, soursop or other fruit juices. Sunday dinner was always scheduled for no later than 3:00 p.m. Dessert, a slice of Sweet Potato Pudding or Cornmeal Pone, was usually eaten later, with a hot beverage, just before retiring for the night.

The recipes in this cookbook were the basis of many happy meals from my childhood and adult years. My mother made them for us, and I have since shared these meals with my own family and friends. The intent of this cookbook is to share the strong tradition of down-to-earth Jamaican cooking, as passed down from my mother to me.

# A BRIEF HISTORY OF JAMAICAN CUISINE

"Out of Many, One People" is the national motto of Jamaica, in recognition of the diverse ethnic origins of its present day inhabitants. It is a cultural heritage reflected in the island's colourful cuisine.

Following the near extinction of the indigenous Arawak Indians, Jamaica was predominantly settled by the peoples of Africa, Europe, India, and China. Later, immigrants from the Middle East, North and South America and other parts of the Caribbean also contributed to the cultural motif. With each new group of settlers, arrived unique and exotic blends of spices and flavourings. Individual cultures and dishes intermingled to develop what is today considered traditional Jamaican fare. As the twenty-first century unfolds, Jamaica society has become increasingly influenced by its dominant neighbour, the U.S.A. Commercial hamburgers, fried chicken and pizzas are now competing with the more traditional Jamaican Beef Patties, Fish and Bammies.

The broad range of Jamaican dishes reflects its diverse cultural history. Jerked meats, one of the better known island specialities, originated with the Maroons. Curried Goat and Mango Chutney came from India; Shrimp and Rice, Sweet and Sour Pork, and Peppered Steak from the Chinese; Escoveitch Fish and dishes such as Stewed Peas, Oxtail and Beans, Cow's foot and Beans had Spanish origins. Fricasseed Chicken, Jamaican Beef Soup and Beef Patty were believed to have originated with the French; Run Down, Turned Cornmeal, Dukunoo and Fufu hailed from Africa, while Roast Beef, corned or salted beef, and salted codfish became standard fare under the British.

Jamaica has often been described as the Garden or Orchard of the West Indies, due to the abundance and variety of plant life that carpets the island. Many of these plants are not native to Jamaica, but were introduced by the various inhabitants since colonization. Jamaican cuisine depends upon a complex cornucopia of vegetables including callaloo (one of Jamaica's most

loved vegetables), cassava, sweet potatoes, yams, corn, red peas (kidney beans), okra, pumpkins, ackee, cabbage, breadfruit, cocos, plantains, cho chos, peppers, and many many more. Some of the most commonly eaten fruits include bananas, avocados, pineapples, mangoes, papayas, citruses, and coconuts. Jamaicans have developed a renewed sense of pride and interest in their traditional cuisine. Some foods that were historically considered inferior have now regained their rightful place in the kitchen.

This book is dedicated to the women of Jamaica, who for generations have performed culinary miracles on their raised fireplaces. With one or two iron pots as their main utensils, they established a uniquely flavourful cuisine which has gained unprecedented popularity far beyond the beautiful white sands and blue waters of the island called JAMAICA.

# APPETIZERS
# &
# SNACKS

# APPETIZERS & SNACKS

A s a rule, I do not prepare appetizers. My main courses are usually time-consuming and filling. I like to serve a cocktail before a meal, which almost immediately enhances my guests' anticipation of the enjoyable meal awaiting them. For a lunch or brunch, which is less time-consuming, appetizers and snacks are a **must**.

Jamaican Beef Patties...10

Codfish Balls...12

Mom's Codfish Fritters...13

Crab Fritters...14

Cocktail Meatballs...15

Solomon Gundy Spread....16

Eggs Stuffed with Crabmeat....17

Seafood Spread....18

Plantain Chips...18

Tomato Dip...19

Avocado Dip...20

# JAMAICAN BEEF PATTIES

In Canada, in 1985, the Jamaican Patty gained notoriety in the Province of Ontario. It was somehow decided that the 'Jamaican Beef Patty' was not a patty at all because it had a 'crust'. In that case, it was said to be a 'beef pie' and it had to be advertised as such. All major patty outlets were warned by Consumer and Corporate Affairs Canada – the agency which enforces the federal Food and Drug Act – that they could face a $5,000 fine if they did not change the label to 'beef pie'. The 'Patty War' was declared! Many people came to the defense of the 'Jamaican Patty'. Roy Williams, then President of the Jamaican Canadian Association, said "The patty is indigenous to the culture of Jamaicans; it is a part of Jamaican ethnic cuisine known the world over and we will never give up the label of 'Beef Patty'." The ministry was forced to surrender. Since that time, millions of Jamaican Beef Patties have been sold throughout Canada every year. They are available frozen, freshly baked in Jamaican bakeries, and are sold in restaurants and snack bars.

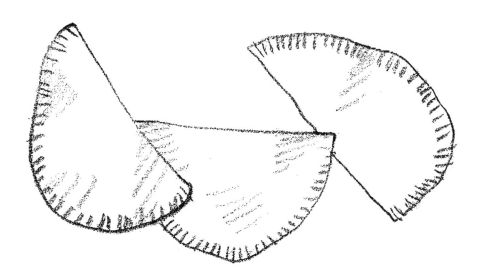

# JAMAICAN BEEF PATTIES

**Filling for Patties**

1 lb ground beef
1 onion, finely chopped
  or grated
2 stalks scallion, finely
  chopped
¼ cup cooking oil
1 Scotch Bonnet
  pepper minced,
  seeds removed
1 cup bread crumbs
½ teaspoon thyme
  leaves
1 tablespoon curry
  powder
¼ teaspoon salt
½ teaspoon black
  pepper
½ cup water

1. Combine the ground beef, chopped onion, scallion and Scotch bonnet pepper, mix well.
2. Heat the oil in a frying pan and add the meat mixture.
3. Stir frequently while cooking for about 10 minutes until liquid is absorbed.
4. Pour off excess oil.
5. Combine the breadcrumbs, thyme, curry powder, salt and pepper with the meat mixture.
6. Add the water, cover and simmer for 30 minutes.
7. The mixture should be moist but with very little oil.
8. Remove from heat and cool to room temperature.

**Pastry for Patties**

2 cups flour
½ tablespoon curry
  powder
½ teaspoon salt
½ cup margarine
Cold water

1. Combine flour, curry powder and salt.
2. Mix in the margarine.
3. Add cold water (about 3-6 tablespoons at a time) to hold the dough into a ball.
4. Wrap in foil paper and chill 15-20 minutes for easier rolling.
5. Separate the dough into 12 pieces.

Sprinkle flour on each piece and roll into a circle the size of a saucer.

6. Place enough filling on one half of each circle.

7. Fold the other half over and seal edges by crimping them with a fork.

8. Bake the patties on ungreased baking sheets in a preheated oven at 400° F for 20-30 minutes or until golden brown.

Makes about 1 dozen patties.

NOTE: For cocktail sized patties reduce the size of the pastry circle and the portion of the filling. Spear with cocktail picks and serve on a platter. Patties are best when served hot.

# CODFISH BALLS

*My friends usually request that I "bring the Codfish Balls" to their parties. These are very popular so make sure you make enough to go around!*

½ lb salted codfish (preferably boneless)

4 medium sized potatoes

1 onion, finely minced or grated

¼ teaspoon black pepper

Few pieces of Scotch Bonnet pepper, finely chopped (discard seeds)

1 teaspoon thyme leaves

2 eggs, beaten

Cooking oil for frying

1. Soak the codfish overnight.
2. Next day discard the water and place the fish in a saucepan with fresh water.
3. Peel, wash and chop the potatoes into pieces.
4. Cook with the fish until the potatoes are tender, drain off water.
5. Remove the skin and bones of the fish if it is not boneless.
6. With a potato masher or fork, mash together the fish, potatoes, grated onion, Scotch Bonnet pepper and add black pepper and thyme.
7. Cool slightly.
8. Add the beaten eggs and beat all the ingredients together.
9. Use a teaspoon to form the mixture into balls. Deep fry in hot oil until golden brown.

Spear with cocktail picks and serve warm. Makes 24 balls.

# MOM'S CODFISH FRITTERS

*This was one of my favourite Sunday morning breakfasts. On Sunday mornings before church, my mother served this with hard dough bread and a hot beverage of cocoa or chocolate. Church services were quite lengthy so she made sure we had a full stomach before going.*

½ lb salted codfish
3 cups flour
1 medium sized onion grated, or finely chopped
1 teaspoon paprika or annato (for colouring)
Few pieces of Scotch Bonnet pepper finely chopped (discard seeds)
1 teaspoon baking powder
¼ teaspoon black pepper
¼ teaspoon thyme leaves
Cooking oil for frying

1. Soak the codfish in cold water at least 4 hours.
2. Drain off water.
3. To avoid excessive saltiness, add fresh water and boil for 10 minutes.
4. Drain and when cool remove skin and bones.
5. Place the codfish in a mixing bowl and shred finely.
6. Add the balance of ingredients and enough water to make a batter similar to that of pancakes, but not as runny.
7. Have a skillet well heated with oil for frying, using a moderate amount of oil.
8. Fry the batter in spoonfuls as you would for pancakes. Space well apart and turn until they are golden brown on each side.
9. Place the fried fritters on paper towels to absorb excess oil.

Serve immediately or place in a warm oven until ready to serve.
Makes 10-12 fritters

# CRAB FRITTERS

1 lb cooked crab meat,
   fresh or canned
1 small onion, finely
   chopped
1 tablespoon chopped
   parsley
3 eggs, beaten
¼ cup breadcrumbs
Salt and pepper to
   taste
2 tablespoons
   vegetable oil

1. Combine seasonings, beaten eggs and crab meat.
2. Add enough breadcrumbs to bind the mixture.
3. Shape into fritters and fry lightly until golden brown.

Serve immediately.
Makes 12 Fritters.

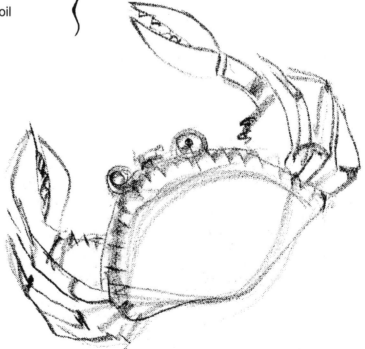

# COCKTAIL MEATBALLS

2 lbs ground beef
1 onion, grated
1 clove garlic, grated
1 teaspoon salt
2 tablespoons finely
   chopped parsley
   (optional)
1 egg
½ teaspoon thyme
¾ cup white wine
2 tablespoons
   vegetable oil

1. Combine all ingredients (except the vegetable oil) with ¼ cup of the white wine.
2. Mix well.
3. Form small portions into walnut shapes and place them on an oiled baking pan.
4. Bake for 20 minutes in a preheated oven at 475°F.
5. Remove from the oven. Place the balls in an ovenproof dish then add the rest of the wine and the pan juices.
6. Return meatballs to oven and keep warm.

Makes 24 meat balls.

# SOLOMON GUNDY SPREAD

*Because of its saltiness, people with high blood pressure should avoid eating excessive amounts of this spread. It is hard to resist!*

2 lbs pickled shad
½ lb pickled mackerel
1 tablespoon vinegar
⅓ cup vegetable oil
1 tablespoon pimento seeds (whole allspice)
4 stalks scallion, finely chopped
A very small amount each of minced green, yellow and red Scotch Bonnet pepper to make an attractive contrast
1 medium sized onion, finely chopped

1. Place all the fish in a large bowl of cold water and soak for at least 4 hours to remove excess salt. Discard water.
2. Soak for another 10 minutes in enough boiling water to cover. Discard the water.
3. Remove heads, skin and bones and shred the flesh into small pieces.
4. Place shredded fish in a bowl and add the chopped onions, scallions, peppers, vinegar, pimento seeds, and oil. Mix well.
5. Allow to stand overnight before serving. Do not refrigerate.

The spread can be stored in a jar and refrigerated after 24 hours.
Serve as a snack on unsalted crackers.

# EGGS STUFFED WITH CRABMEAT

½ cup crabmeat
6 hard-boiled eggs
½ stalk celery, finely
   chopped
1 tablespoon
   mayonnaise
1 clove garlic, finely
   chopped
¼ teaspoon chopped
   parsley
Salt to taste
½ teaspoon freshly
   ground black pepper
1 teaspoon dry mustard
Dash of Pickapeppa or
   Tabasco sauce

1. Shred the crabmeat, discard any shells or
   cartilage.
2. Peel the eggs and cut in half lengthwise.
3. Mash the yolks in a medium bowl, set
   whites aside.
4. Add remaining ingredients to the yolks
   and mix well.
5. Stuff each egg-white with crabmeat filling.
6. Cover and refrigerate until chilled before
   serving.

Makes 6 servings.

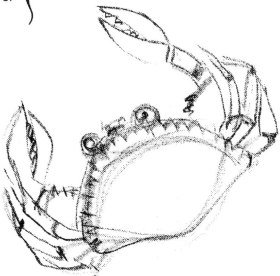

# SEAFOOD SPREAD

8 oz cream cheese
½ cup each cooked
  crab, shrimp and
  lobster
1 teaspoon Pickapeppa
  or Tabasco sauce
¼ teaspoon black
  pepper
2 tablespoons milk
1 teaspoon finely
  chopped parsley
Crackers for serving

1. Beat the cream cheese until smooth.
2. Add the next 5 ingredients and mix well.

Serve on crackers.
Makes 24 servings.

# PLANTAIN CHIPS

2 green plantains
Pinch of salt
Cooking oil for frying

1. Peel the plantains and slice thinly into rings. Soak in salted water for 30 minutes.
2. Drain well and dry with paper towels.
3. Fry quickly in hot oil until golden brown.
4. Place on paper towels to absorb excess oil.

Serve warm.
Makes 2-4 servings.

# TOMATO DIP

*This is delicious with raw vegetables.*

½ cup tomato ketchup

¼ teaspoon garlic powder

1½ tablespoons green onions or scallions finely chopped

1½ teaspoons granulated sugar

½ teaspoon lime juice

¼ teaspoon salt

¼ teaspoon black pepper

1. Place all the ingredients in a blender and mix for 30 seconds.

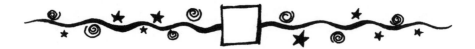

# AVOCADO DIP

1 small, ripe avocado
   pear
1 small tomato
1 small onion, chopped
1 tablespoon lime juice
½ teaspoon salt
¼ teaspoon black
   pepper
1 teaspoon chili powder
2 stalks celery, finely
   chopped

1. Peel and seed the pear.
2. Chop the flesh coarsely.
3. Remove the skin from the tomato, chop the flesh.
4. Place all ingredients in a blender and blend for 30 seconds. If a blender is not available use a fork or a potato masher to mash the ingredients.

Serve immediately as a dip or salad dressing.

# SOUPS

# SOUPS

Jamaican soups are thick and rich enough to be eaten as a meal. They can be made from beef bones or beef shank, oxtail, pig's tail or salt beef. Various vegetables are added: callaloo, kale, pumpkin, carrots, turnips, cho chos, peas and beans — depending on the kind of soup. If the soup is to be served as a main course meal, yams, cocos, breadfruit or dumplings are added. Their wonderful flavour comes from the seasoning of garlic, scallion, fresh thyme, black pepper and unbroken Scotch bonnet pepper.

The ingredients required to make the following soups are easily available in Jamaican and other West Indian food stores. In Toronto, one of the most popular places to shop for West Indian food is the Kensington Market.

Jamaican Red Pea Soup...23

Spinners (Dumplings)...24

Gungo Pea Soup...24

Fish Tea or Soup...25

Oliver's Mannish Water...26

Jamaican Pepperpot soup...28

Pumpkin Soup...30

# JAMAICAN RED PEA SOUP

*Red peas (kidney beans) are one of the most popular peas in Jamaica. This soup is usually served as a main dish and can be quite filling. If served as an appetizer, eliminate the dumplings and yams.*

1½ lbs beef shank or stewing beef

1 lb pig's tail (optional)

1 lb salt beef, soaked overnight to avoid excess saltiness

1 clove garlic, crushed

2 cups dried red peas (kidney beans), soaked overnight

8 cups water

1 lb coco peeled, washed and diced

1 lb yellow yam or other hard yam, peeled, washed and diced

1 lb sweet potatoes, peeled, washed and diced

Spinners (see recipe page 24)

3 stalks scallion, crushed

1 sprig fresh thyme

Black pepper

1 whole unbroken Scotch Bonnet pepper

1. Wash the meats and put them in a large pot with the water.
2. Add the garlic and peas and bring to the boil.
3. Cook until meats are nearly tender. Skim off the froth as it rises.
4. Add the sweet potatoes, yam, cocos and spinners.
5. Add more boiling water to make up to 8 cups.
6. When ingredients are almost cooked add scallion, thyme, black pepper and unbroken Scotch Bonnet pepper.
7. Stir and taste for flavour, add salt if necessary.
8. Simmer for another 10 minutes. The soup should be moderately thick.

Before serving remove the whole hot pepper, being careful not to break it.

Makes 6-8 servings.

# SPINNERS (DUMPLINGS)

2 cups flour

¼ cup cornmeal
(optional)

¼ teaspoon salt

Cold water

1. Combine flour, cornmeal, and salt.
2. Add water (a little at a time) and knead until smooth.
3. Break off small pieces from the dough.
4. Rub between your palms to make 1" cylinder-shaped spinners.

# GUNGO PEAS SOUP

*The gungo pea is known by various other names including congo and pigeon pea and is one of the most loved peas in Jamaica. As a variation of the Red Peas Soup, green gungo peas can be substituted for the Red Peas. The other ingredients and method are the same.*

# FISH TEA OR SOUP

*In some rural areas in Jamaica the word 'tea' is used to describe any non-alcoholic hot drink. Breakfast is still referred to as 'tea' in some areas.*

1 lb fish head (preferably grouper, kingfish or whole doctor fish)
10 cups water
2 Irish (white) potatoes, peeled and diced
2 carrots, peeled and diced
1 cho cho, peeled and diced
2 small turnips, peeled and diced
2 green bananas, sliced (one with skin left on)
2 stalks scallion or green onions
Few pimento seeds
2 sprigs thyme
1 whole Scotch Bonnet pepper
¼ teaspoon salt
¼ teaspoon black pepper
1 pack chicken noodle soup mix (optional)

1. Clean and wash the fish well.
2. Bring the water to a boil in a large pot.
3. Add the fish and reduce heat to medium.
4. Simmer for 30 minutes or until the flesh begins to separate from the bones.
5. Add the rest of the ingredients and more water to cover.
6. Simmer for 40 minutes. Remove hot pepper.

Serve hot.
Makes 6 servings.

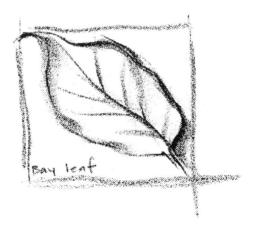

Bay leaf

# OLIVER'S MANNISH WATER

*I gave this soup the name of my brother, Oliver, because when he came from Jamaica to Toronto to attend a festive occasion he was assigned the task of making the 'mannish water'. It is claimed, by some Jamaican men, that mannish water has aphrodisiac properties. All I can say is this soup is absolutely delicious!*

*Mannish water is always cooked in large amounts to feed at least 25 people.*

4 lbs each goat head, tripe, and feet. (Goat head is pre-cleaned and sold in meat shops. Ask the butcher to chop the head and feet in pieces).

12 cups water

1 dozen green bananas, sliced in thin rings, do not peel

1 lb Irish (white) potatoes, peeled and diced

1 cho cho, peeled and diced

1 lb carrots, scraped, washed and diced

1. Wash meats thoroughly. Cut the tripe into small pieces.
2. Pour the 12 cups of water in a large pot and bring to boil.
3. Add meats, and crushed garlic. Cook for 2 hours or until meats are tender. Remove bones.
4. Add spinners, potatoes, bananas, cho cho, carrots and salt. Add more water if necessary.
5. Simmer for 1 hour on medium heat.
6. Add pimento seeds, scallion, thyme, chicken noodle soup mix, whole Scotch Bonnet peppers, and black pepper.
7. Simmer for another 30 minutes, stir occasionally to keep vegetables and meats from sticking to the pot.
8. Remove the hot peppers (some Jamaicans prefer their mannish water hot with pepper, if so, burst 1 pepper into the soup and discard the other 2).

Spinners (see recipe
   page 24)
½ tablespoon salt
3 doz pimento seeds
12 stalks scallion or
   green onion
8 sprigs thyme
3 packs chicken noodle
   soup mix (optional)
3 Scotch Bonnet
   peppers, unbroken
Black pepper to taste
1 cup white Jamaican
   rum (optional)

9. Add rum (optional).

Serve hot in cups.
Makes 25 servings.

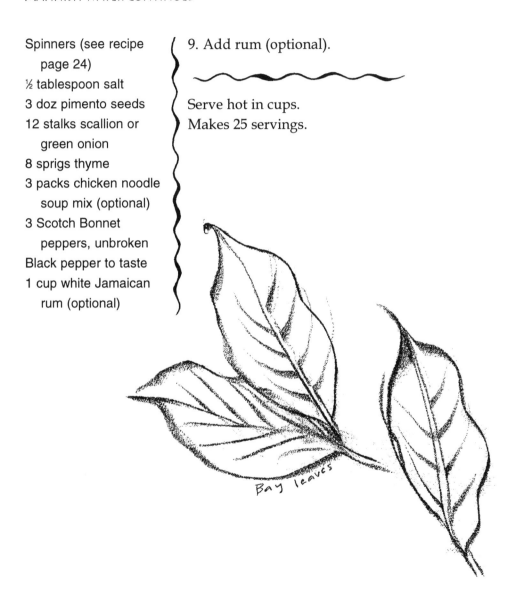

Bay leaves

# JAMAICAN PEPPERPOT SOUP

*There is hardly a Jamaican who has not had pepperpot soup. It is believed that this soup originated with the Arawak Indians who passed the recipe on to the African slaves. In the past it had the thicker consistency of a stew. It is often confused with another well-known dish, the Guyanese "Pepperpot" made from mixed meats, seasonings and cassareep. In Jamaica the ingredients have varied according to what is available. Shrimp can also be added to this delicious hot dish.*

10 cups water

½ lb beef shank or stewing beef

2 cloves garlic, crushed

1 lb salted pig's tail, could be soaked beforehand to remove excess salt

1 lb spinach or callaloo, washed and chopped

1 dozen okras, washed and sliced into rings

½ lb each coco, yellow yam, and sweet potato, peeled, sliced and washed

1 whole cho cho (Chayote), peeled, sliced and washed

Black pepper to taste

1. Bring the water to a boil in a large pot.
2. Add the beef, pig's tail and crushed garlic.
3. Cook for 45 minutes or until the meats are tender.
4. Add the okras, coco, yam, sweet potato, cho cho, callaloo (or spinach) and dumplings.
5. Simmer for 30 minutes or until the yams and cocos are tender.
6. Add the coconut milk, crushed scallion, thyme and unbroken Scotch Bonnet pepper.
7. Add more water if necessary.
8. Stir occasionally to keep ingredients from sticking to the pot.
9. Simmer for another 20 minutes until the soup has thickened.

Spinners (see recipe
   page 24)
3 cups coconut milk
3 large stalks scallion,
   crushed
1 whole unbroken
   Scotch Bonnet
   pepper
1 or 2 sprigs fresh
   thyme
Black pepper to taste

Makes 6-8 servings

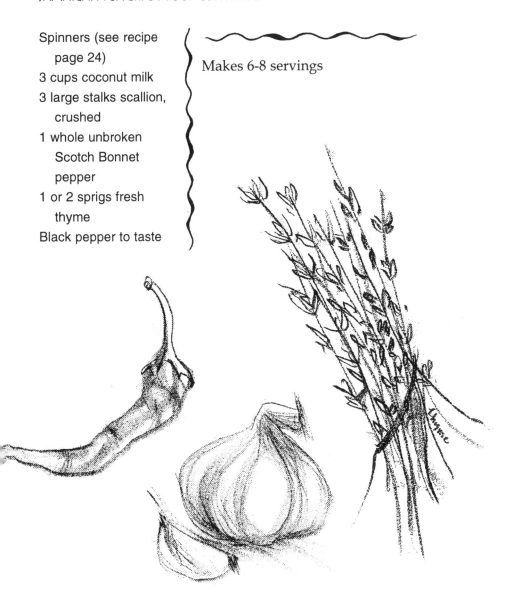

thyme

# PUMPKIN SOUP

*For the best flavour use Caribbean pumpkin, also known in Spanish as "Calabaza".*

8 cups water
1½ lbs stewing beef
¾ lb lean salt beef or
    pickled pig's tail
2 lbs pumpkin (bright
    & yellow inside),
    diced
2 cocos, peeled and
    diced
1 lb yellow yam or
    other hard yam,
    peeled and diced
2 large stalks scallion,
    crushed
1 whole clove garlic,
    crushed
1 whole unbroken
    Scotch Bonnet
    pepper
2 sprigs thyme

1. Bring the water to boil in a large pot.
2. Add the stewing beef, pig's tail or salt beef and crushed garlic.
3. Cover the pot and simmer until the meat is fairly tender.
4. Add the diced pumpkin, cocos and yam. Add more water if necessary.
5. Simmer until the yam and cocos are tender and the pumpkin is soft.
6. Add the scallion, thyme and whole pepper, taste for salt.
7. Stir and simmer for 5 minutes.

Serve piping hot

NOTE: The pickled or salted meat should add sufficient salt to this soup. No salt should be added until soup is nearly cooked.

Makes 6 servings.

# MEAT,
# POULTRY
# & GAME

Ossie's Jerk Pit

# MEAT DISHES

Meats are usually seasoned and left to marinate for at least 2 hours before cooking. They are slowly cooked, producing a tenderness that hardly needs a knife to cut it. Instant gravy mixes are seldom used. Instead, the drippings together with the seasonings and a little water are used to produce a rich and preservative-free gravy. Fresh or frozen, fricasseed, jerked, baked, fried, roasted, barbecued, grilled, as a light lunch or a family feast, chicken's easy-going nature is just right for anytime. Chicken is easy on the budget, easy on the timetable, and ever-so-easy on the taste buds. Chicken, particularly skinless, is one of the leanest meats around.

Jamaican Fricassed Chicken...33
Curried Chicken...34
Chicken Cooked in Sweet Peas and Carrots...35
Curried Rabbit...36
Quick Jerk Pork...38
Jerk Pork...39
Jerk Pork Chops on the Barbeque...40
Jerk Chicken...41
Curried Goat...42
Spiced Braised Beef with Tomatoes...44
Beef and Okra...45
Beef Balls...46
Beef Stewed in Red Stripe Beer...47
Pineapple Spareribs...48
Pepper Steak – Jamaican-Chinese Style...49
Chinese Jamaican Chop Suey...50
Chinese Gingered Pork....51
Chinese Honey Garlic Chicken Wings...52

# JAMAICAN FRICASSEED CHICKEN

*The secret of fricasseed chicken, a great Jamaican sensation, is in the marinade, a seasoning of onion, garlic, Scotch Bonnet pepper, salt and black pepper.*

1 chicken, cut in approximately 12 pieces
1 fairly large onion, coarsely chopped
2 cloves garlic, finely chopped
1 teaspoon black pepper
½ teaspoon salt
1 large tomato, chopped
2 sprigs thyme
A few pieces of Scotch Bonnet pepper (discard seeds)
½ cup cooking oil
1 cup water

1. Rinse chicken pieces with vinegar and water. Dry with paper towel.
2. Place in a bowl and rub with the first 7 ingredients, working the herbs and spices into the chicken flesh.
3. Cover and leave to marinate overnight in the refrigerator or for 4 hours.
4. Next day scrape off the onion, tomatoes, thyme, garlic and retain with the marinade.
5. Heat oil in a heavy saucepan or Dutch pot. Fry chicken pieces until golden brown. Drain off oil.
6. Add the seasonings, marinade and 1 cup of water.
7. Cover pot and simmer for 45 minutes or until the chicken is tender and the gravy reaches a desired consistency.
8. Taste for flavour, add more salt and black pepper if necessary.

Serve with rice and peas, fried plantains and a fresh salad.
Soursop or carrot juice are drinks that complement this dish.
Makes 4-5 servings

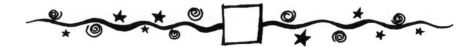

# CURRIED CHICKEN

1 chicken
½ teaspoon salt
¼ teaspoon black pepper
2 tablespoons curry powder
1 onion, coarsely chopped
3 cloves garlic, minced
1 Scotch Bonnet pepper finely chopped (discard seeds)
2 sprigs or ½ teaspoon thyme leaves
2 bay leaves
1 stalk scallion or green onion, crushed
¼ cup cooking oil
1 cup water

1. Cut chicken in serving sized pieces and wash with vinegar or lime juice.
2. Rub the first 9 ingredients thoroughly into chicken, cover and leave to marinate for 1-2 hours.
3. Heat oil in a deep saucepan.
4. Scrape off the seasonings, retain with the marinade.
5. Fry chicken on both sides until golden brown. Pour off the oil.
6. Add the seasonings, marinade, and 1 cup water.
7. Simmer until the chicken is tender and the gravy reaches a desired thickness. The gravy should be nice and rich — but not oily.

Serve on a bed of piping hot cooked rice or boiled green bananas and a fresh salad.
Makes 4-5 servings

# CHICKEN COOKED IN SWEET PEAS AND CARROTS

*This recipe was given to me by one of my friends in Toronto. I have tried it and it's absolutely delicious.*

1 medium chicken cut into pieces, and skinned. Use the legs, thighs and breasts and save the back and wings for stock.
¼ cup cooking oil
1 large onion, thinly sliced
2 cloves garlic, minced
Black pepper to taste
½ teaspoon thyme leaves
1½ cups sliced carrots
½ cup fresh sweet peas (if not available the frozen ones can be substituted)
2 cups water

1. Wash chicken pieces in water to which vinegar or lime juice has been added.
2. Dry chicken pieces on paper towel.
3. Place chicken in a bowl, add the seasonings and marinate for 1 hour.
4. Remove the seasonings and retain.
5. Brown chicken pieces in hot oil in a deep saucepan.
6. Pour off excess oil.
7. Place seasonings and marinade in the pot with the chicken, cover with 2 cups of boiling water and bring to the boil.
8. Lower heat and simmer for 30 minutes or until the chicken is tender.
9. Add carrots and peas and simmer for another 20 minutes until the vegetables are tender and the sauce reaches the desired consistency.

Serve with mashed potatoes or boiled rice and a fresh crisp salad.
Makes 4 servings

# CURRIED RABBIT

*This dish is absolutely delicious. Curried rabbit meat has an identical taste to curried chicken and it is difficult to differentiate one from the other. Rabbit meat is very nutritious and low in fat content.*

3 lbs rabbit, cut in serving pieces

1 medium onion, chopped

3 cloves garlic, minced

3 tablespoons curry powder

1 teaspoon salt

½ teaspoon black pepper

1 tomato, chopped

2 sprigs fresh or dried thyme

3 bay leaves

Few pieces of Scotch Bonnet pepper

1½ cups water

2 tablespoons cooking oil

1. Rinse rabbit pieces with vinegar and water. Pat dry.
2. Combine first 10 ingredients in a bowl (all except water and oil) and rub into the meat. Marinate 2-3 hours.
3. Heat the oil in a saucepan or Dutch pot.
4. Scrape seasonings from meat and reserve with the marinade.
5. Cook meat in batches until golden brown, adding more oil if necessary.
6. When all the pieces are brown remove and set aside.
7. Pour off the oil and add 1½ cups water.
8. Add the seasonings and marinade, bring to a boil.
9. Return the meat to the saucepan and reduce heat to medium.
10. Simmer for 30 minutes or until the meat is tender. Add more salt or seasonings, if required.
11. Simmer until the gravy reaches the desired consistency. Do not use cornstarch or flour to thicken the gravy as this will alter the flavour tremendously.

CURRIED RABBIT CONTINUED

Freshly grated bread will add both flavour and thickness.

Serve with rice and peas, and a fresh salad. Makes 4-6 servings.

## WHERE'S THE JERK?

My first taste of jerked pork was in 1978 when I visited Jamaica. We drove from Kingston to Boston in Portland where jerked pork originated. The taste was overwhelming and the experience unforgettable.

Jerked meat is indigenous to Jamaica and has a fascinating history. It is thought to have originated with the Caribs and Arawaks, the aboriginal peoples of the Caribbean. The tradition was carried on by the Maroons, runaway slaves who settled in remote mountainous areas of Jamaica.

To jerk pork, a pit is dug and in which a fire is made mainly with the wood of the pimento tree. A grill is made from sticks standing about 1 foot above the fire pit. The meat is rubbed with seasonings and left to marinate for hours or sometimes days. The meat is placed on the grill, under which a slow fire is kept burning until the meat is cooked. It is the seasoning, the length of time the meat is marinated, and the smoke from the leaves and sticks which contribute to the unique flavour of jerked meat.

We might not have a pit or pimento wood in Canada, but we have lots of seasonings to make it jerk! There are several brands of jerk seasonings available in Jamaican and West Indian food stores in Toronto. I have experimented with a few brands but I also make my own concoction because it's fresh and contains very little preservatives. However, one tablespoon of commercial jerk seasoning could be added to your homemade concoction, if you prefer spicier seasoning.

# VERSION 1: QUICK JERK PORK

*This version is super easy and can be prepared in less than two hours.*

**Jerk Seasoning**

4 Scotch Bonnet peppers, chopped, seeds removed

1 tablespoon Jamaican whole pimento berries

2 large cloves garlic, chopped

8 stalks scallion, chopped

1 large onion, chopped

1 teaspoon salt

½ teaspoon whole black peppercorns

1 tablespoon thyme leaves

¼ cup mushroom sauce

¼ cup red wine vinegar

1 teaspoon cloves

1 tablespoon brown sugar

4 pounds boneless pork shoulder roast, unskinned (do not cut)

2 dozen whole pimento berries

4 bay leaves

1. To make the Jerk Seasoning place the first 12 ingredients in a food processor, fitted with a steel blade. Grind for 5-8 seconds until smooth.

2. In a large pot bring to boil enough water to cover pork. Add two dozen pimento seeds and bay leaves. Do not add salt.

3. Add the pork and par-boil for 20 minutes.

4. Remove the pork from the water, set aside to cool and discard the water.

5. When pork is cool, chop into serving-size pieces.

6. Pour the seasoning over the meat and coat thoroughly.

7. Cover to marinate for at least 1 hour, turning occasionally.

8. Remove the pork pieces from the marinade and place in a roasting pan. Reserve the marinade for basting. Cover and cook in a preheated oven at 375°F for 30 minutes.

9. Remove cover and cook for another half hour. Brush the meat with the marinade and continue cooking, turning and basting with the pan dripping until tender.

10. Remove the meat and place in an oven proof dish to keep warm.

Serve with steaming rice and peas and a fresh salad.

Makes 4-6 Servings

Store left-over seasoning in a jar for future use.

# VERSION 2: JERK PORK

4 lbs boneless pork shoulder, unskinned

1. Wash and score pork with a knife every half inch.
2. Pour the seasoning mixture over the pork and rub it in well. Cover and refrigerate overnight turning occasionally.
3. Roast at 325° F for approximately 2 hours. Baste continually until cooked.
4. Remove from oven, let sit for 10-15 minutes then slice and serve.

# JERK PORK CHOPS ON A BARBEQUE GRILL

*In Jamaica green pimento leaves or sticks are thrown on the burning charcoal to give the meat the required taste and aroma. Those of us abroad can substitute the pimento leaves with bay leaves and pimento berries thrown onto the burning charcoal to create an authentic flavour.*

4 lbs pork chops or any other cut.

1. Prepare the jerk seasoning in the same manner as on page 38.
2. Wash the chops and rub with jerk seasoning.
3. Marinate for 2 hours or overnight.
4. Scrape off seasonings.
5. Gently cook the chops on the grill of a charcoal barbeque.
6. Turn over when one side is done. The chops should be ready in 1 hour.

Makes 10-12 servings

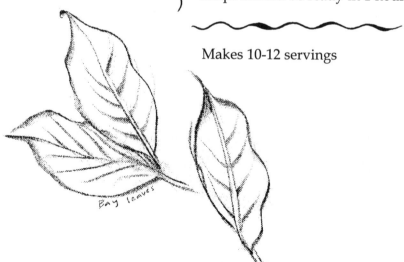

Bay leaves

# JERKED CHICKEN

1 whole chicken, skin
removed

1. Cut the chicken into serving-sized pieces and wash in water to which vinegar or lime juice has been added.
2. Place the chicken in a bowl and rub with the jerk seasoning. Cover and marinate for at least 2 hours. Preheat oven to 325° F.
3. Remove the chicken pieces from the marinade and place in a roasting pan.
4. Cover and roast for 1 hour until the juice is almost gone. Remove the cover and allow to brown, turning occasionally. When the chicken is cooked the meat should easily separate from the bones.

Makes 4 servings

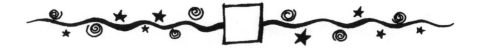

# CURRIED GOAT

*Curried Goat, another national dish of Jamaica, is served on special occasions such as weddings or large house parties. It is believed that the Indians who came to Jamaica as indentured workers from 1842 onwards, used the following method to produce this dish. The goat meat has a unique flavour and is milder than lamb meat.*

*A friend of mine, from Germany, told me that he had never dreamed he would ever eat goat meat. He was pleasantly surprised at the splendid flavour! To eliminate excess fat, I do not brown the meat in oil. The curry provides ample colour and flavour.*

2 lbs goat meat
1 teaspoon salt
½ teaspoon black pepper
3 tablespoons curry powder
2 cloves garlic, finely chopped
1 onion, finely chopped
1 stalk scallion, chopped
2 bay leaves
1 Scotch Bonnet pepper, chopped (with or without seeds)
2 sprigs thyme or 1 teaspoon thyme leaves
2½ cups water

1. Wash and cut the meat into bite-sized pieces.
2. Leave in the bones as they add flavour and become chewable after cooking.
3. Combine seasoning ingredients and rub them into the meat (I usually wear rubber gloves to protect my hands from the pepper and the smell of seasoning).
4. Cover and marinate overnight or for at least 1½ hours.
5. Bring the water to boil in a Dutch pot or heavy saucepan. Add the goat meat, the seasonings and the marinade, stir.
6. Cover the pot and cook slowly over medium heat, stir occasionally.
7. Continue to simmer for at least 1-2 hours or until the meat is tender and easily separates from the bones. Add more water if necessary.

8. Taste and correct the seasoning. If the gravy is too thin, increase heat and reduce the liquid to desired consistency or add a little freshly grated bread crumbs. Remove bay leaves before serving.

Serve on top of piping hot boiled rice, or boiled green bananas with a fresh salad. Makes 4-6 servings.

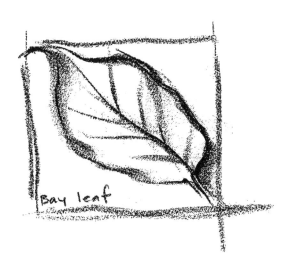

Bay leaf

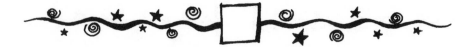

# JAMAICAN SPICED BRAISED BEEF WITH TOMATOES

3 lbs lean chuck steak
Salt and black pepper
   to taste
3 tablespoon cooking
   oil
2 cloves garlic, finely
   chopped
2 medium sized onions,
   thinly sliced in rings
1 cup flour
1 cup dry red wine
   (optional)
2 tomatoes, coarsely
   chopped
1 bay leaf
2 sprigs dried thyme
Pinch of cayenne
¼ cup finely chopped
   parsley

1. Wash the meat, trim off the fat and cut into 1½ inch cubes.
2. Sprinkle cubes with salt and black pepper.
3. Heat oil in a saucepan until quite hot.
4. Brown the beef cubes, stirring often.
5. Stir in the garlic and onions.
6. Sprinkle with flour and stir to coat the pieces evenly.
7. Add the wine, tomatoes, bay leaf, thyme, and cayenne pepper.
8. Stir while bringing to a boil.
9. Cover and simmer slowly until the beef is tender, taste for flavour and add salt and black pepper if necessary.
10. Pour the beef stew into a serving dish, sprinkle with chopped parsley.

Serve with rice and peas, plain rice, or mashed potatoes and a salad.
Makes 6-8 Servings

# BEEF & OKRA

*Cabbage, carrots or turnips add super flavour to this meat dish.*

3 lbs beef round steak
¼ teaspoon salt
1/4 teaspoon black
  pepper
2 onions, sliced in rings
2 cloves garlic, minced
1 sprig thyme, minced
3 tomatoes, coarsely
  chopped
½ cup vegetable oil
5 cups water
1 lb okra, trimmed and
  sliced

1. Wash the meat. Slice thinly, cutting across the grain.
2. Season with onion, garlic, salt, black pepper, and thyme. Marinate for 1 hour.
3. Heat oil in a large skillet or heavy saucepan.
4. Remove the seasonings, retain with marinade.
5. Brown beef slices. Drain oil.
6. Add the water, seasonings, marinade and tomatoes.
7. Bring to a boil, reduce heat, cover pot and simmer for 1½ hours, or until the meat is tender.
8. Add the okras and simmer for 20 minutes.
9. Taste for flavour and add salt and black pepper if necessary.

Makes 6 servings.

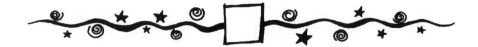

# BEEF BALLS

*This is a very simple but delicious dish. It takes less than an hour to prepare a complete dinner!*

1 lb ground beef
2 eggs, well beaten
½ cup breadcrumbs
   (grated hard dough
   bread)
2 cloves garlic, grated
1 tablespoon onion,
   grated
¼ teaspoon black
   pepper
¼ teaspoon salt
¾ cup cooking oil

**Gravy for Beef Balls**
1 cup water
1 medium onion, sliced
   in rings
1 medium sized
   tomato, coarsely
   chopped
½ medium green
   pepper chopped,
   seeds removed
Pinch of thyme leaves

1. Combine the beef, breadcrumbs, seasonings and beaten eggs.
2. Form the mixture into balls.
3. Heat oil in saucepan and brown.
4. Remove them from the pan and set aside.

**To make the gravy**

5. Bring the water to boil in a saucepan.
6. Add the onion, tomato, green pepper and thyme.
7. Simmer until the vegetables are tender.
8. Return the beef balls to the pan and sprinkle with black pepper. Simmer for about 15 minutes or until the liquid is reduced to about ½ cup.
9. Taste for flavour and add salt and black pepper if necessary.

Serve with rice and peas or plain rice, a green salad or steamed mixed vegetable.
Makes 4-6 servings

# BEEF STEWED IN JAMAICAN RED STRIPE BEER

*It is said that the Red Stripe Beer was named after the red striped seam on the Jamaican police uniform.*

4 bottles Red Stripe Beer (or any commercial beer of your choice)
5 lbs stewing beef, cubed
cooking oil for frying
2 large onions, coarsely chopped
2 cloves garlic, minced
1 sprig thyme
3 stalks scallion or green onion
2 bay leaves
Black pepper to taste
½ cup tomato ketchup
Salt to taste

1. Pour 3 of the bottles of beer into the saucepan. Bring to a boil and reduce to 1¼ cups.
2. Heat the oil in a skillet and brown the beef. Set aside in a dish.
3. In the remaining oil in the skillet, sauté the onions and garlic.
4. Add the thyme, scallion, bay leaves and black pepper. Add the meat and the 1¼ cups of beer. Stir well.
5. Add the remaining bottle of beer and sufficient water to cover the meat.
6. Cover and simmer over medium heat for 1 hour.
7. Add ketchup and salt. Allow to simmer until meat is tender, add more water if necessary.
8. Taste for flavour and correct seasoning if necessary. Serve hot.

Makes 10-12 servings.

# PINEAPPLE SPARERIBS

*Pineapple is called 'pine` in Jamaica and has been grown there for a long time.*

2 lbs spareribs
1 cup canned
   pineapple chunks,
   crushed
⅓ cup soy sauce
3 tablespoons sugar
1 teaspoon grated
   ginger

1. Trim the fat from the ribs.
2. Add ribs to enough boiling water to cover.
3. Parboil for 20 minutes. Remove and set aside to cool.
4. Cut into serving-sized pieces.
5. Place the ribs in a shallow oven proof dish and brush with some of the soya sauce.
6. Bake uncovered in the oven at 325° F for 30 minutes.
7. Combine the pineapple with the remaining soya sauce, sugar and ginger.
8. Spread evenly over the ribs and continue baking uncovered until ribs are tender.

Makes 3-4 servings

# PEPPER STEAK — JAMAICAN-CHINESE STYLE

½ lb lean beef
1 tablespoon soya sauce
1 tablespoon sherry or red wine (optional)
½ teaspoon sugar
2 sweet peppers, one green, one red, diced in squares (seeds removed)
1½ tablespoon cooking oil
¼ teaspoon salt

1. Wash and cut the beef into thin strips.
2. Combine soya sauce, sherry and sugar.
3. Pour the mixture on to the beef and toss.
4. Let stand for 15 minutes, turning occasionally.
5. Heat the oil in a skillet, add the peppers and sauté until slightly limp.
6. Remove from the pan and set aside.
7. Brown the beef in the remaining oil.
8. Return the peppers to the pan, add the marinade, sprinkle with salt and cook for another 2 minutes.

Serve immediately with your favourite side dish.
Makes 1-4 servings

# CHINESE-JAMAICAN CHOP SUEY

1 lb chicken breast,
  diced
1 lb lean pork, diced
  (optional)
1 lb shrimp, each
  shrimp cut in half
1 onion, coarsely
  chopped
1 medium cho cho,
  peeled, washed,
  thinly sliced
1 lb cabbage, washed,
  cut in small chunks
½ lb carrots, scraped,
  washed, diced
3 stalks bok choy or
  Chinese greens,
  washed and
  coarsely chopped
1 tablespoon sugar
1 tablespoon soya
  sauce
1 teaspoon corn starch
1 clove garlic, crushed
1 stalk scallion, minced
½ teaspoon
  salt(optional)
Water
Oil for cooking

1. Wash the vegetables and set aside in the refrigerator.
2. Combine the diced pork, chicken, sugar, salt, cornstarch, black pepper, onion, scallion, soya sauce and 2 tablespoons water and set aside.
3. In a very large skillet or wok, heat 2 tablespoons oil to almost boiling point. Add the vegetables and stir fry for 5 minutes or until vegetables are almost cooked but not soggy. Remove from the heat and set aside.
4. In a very large saucepan heat 2 tablespoons oil to almost boiling point. Add the meat and shrimp. Retain the marinade and seasonings.
5. Stir-fry the meat and shrimp for about 5 minutes. Add the steamed vegetables then the marinade and seasoning. Stir.
6. Cover saucepan and steam for another 2 minutes or until the meat and vegetables are cooked but not over-cooked.

Makes 6-8 servings

# CHINESE GINGERED PORK

2 lbs lean pork, washed in lime water, and cubed

Flour for coating

3 tablespoons cooking oil

1 cup chicken stock

2 tablespoons soya sauce

4 tablespoons dry sherry (optional)

1 large onion, coarsely chopped

2 cloves garlic, minced

2 tablespoon sugar

1 teaspoon ground ginger

¼ teaspoon black pepper

1. Wash and dry the pork. Cube and coat with flour.
2. Brown the meat in a large skillet over medium heat.
3. When the meat is brown, blend in the chicken stock, soya sauce, and sherry.
4. Add the onion, garlic, sugar, ginger and pepper. Cover the skillet and simmer for 20 minutes or until the meat is tender.

Serve with rice and peas or plain rice with a nice salad.

Makes 4 servings.

# CHINESE HONEY GARLIC CHICKEN WINGS

2 lbs chicken wings
⅓ cup honey or maple
  syrup
2 tablespoons chicken
  bouillon
2 tablespoons soya
  sauce
½ teaspoon garlic
  powder
¼ teaspoon ground
  ginger

1. Wash the wings, cut into 2 sections and remove tips.
2. Place chicken wings in a single layer in a large baking pan.
3. Bake at 425° F for 10 minutes.
4. Remove from oven, drain fat from pan.
5. In a small bowl, combine the honey, chicken bouillon, soya sauce, garlic and ginger.
6. Pour over wings and bake for 25 minutes until golden and glazed with sauce.

Makes 4-6 servings

# VARIETY MEATS

Variety meats, so called because of the wide variety in this meat group, are also called Offal, derived from the word 'off-fall.'
They are the parts, such as brains, heart, kidney, liver, sweetbreads, tongue, tripe, feet, head, and tail which are cut away from the carcass when it is prepared for sale.

Who would have thought, a decade or two ago, that supermarkets and butcher shops in Canada would stock items such as oxtail, cow's foot, pig's feet and tripe? Up until the early '70s, the slaughter houses in Canada discarded variety meats, except for livers and kidneys.

The consumption of variety meats was probably introduced to Jamaicans by the Europeans during slavery. Cow's tail (or oxtail), cow's foot and tripe are Jamaicans' favourite variety meats. They are usually cooked with lots of seasonings and served as a separate meat dish, accompanied with boiled rice, yams, and boiled green bananas. Soups are also made from cow's foot, oxtail, and tripe. Yams, cho chos, pumpkin, potatoes and dumplings are added to make full course meals.

Most kinds of variety meats are delicious to eat, extremely nutritious, and should be eaten only when very fresh. They may be frozen, but this should be done on the day of purchase and they should be stored in the freezer no more than three months.

Oxtail and Broad Beans..54
Tripe and Beans..55
Cow's Foot and Lima Beans..56

# OXTAIL AND BROAD BEANS

2 lbs oxtail, jointed
½ teaspoon salt
1 teaspoon black
   pepper
2 cloves garlic, crushed
2 tomatoes, coarsely
   chopped
2 small onions, thinly
   sliced
1 sprig thyme
2-3 slices Scotch
   bonnet pepper
   (seeds removed)
2 tablespoons cooking
   oil
5 cups boiling water
1 cup dried broad
   beans, washed

1. Wash the oxtail and trim excess fat. Season with the salt, black pepper, garlic, tomatoes, onion, thyme and Scotch bonnet pepper. Marinate for 1 hour.
2. Remove the seasonings and retain with the marinade.
3. Heat the oil in a heavy saucepan and brown the oxtail. Drain off fat.
4. Add the 5 cups of boiling water and bring to the boil. Lower heat, cover and simmer for 1½ hours until the pieces are partially cooked. Add more water if necessary.
5. Add the broad beans, seasonings and marinade. Stir and simmer for 30-40 minutes or until the beans are tender. The meat should easily separate from the bone and the gravy should be thickened.
6. Taste for flavour and add black pepper if necessary.

Serve with rice.
Makes 4-6 servings.
NOTE: If canned beans are used, drain and combine beans with meat after meat is cooked. Simmer for 5 minutes.

# TRIPE AND BEANS

*Tripe is not everyone's favourite dish, yet it does have its admirers. It is the lining of the stomach of a cow or goat and varies a great deal in texture. The honeycomb tripe is considered the finest. Usually lima beans are used in this recipe.*

2 lbs honeycomb tripe
8 cups water
2 cloves garlic, crushed
1 teaspoon salt
2 tablespoons curry
  powder
1 onion, chopped
2 stalks scallion or
  green onion,
  chopped
1 tomato, coarsely
  chopped
4 slices Scotch bonnet
  pepper, chopped
  (seeds removed)
1 sprig thyme
Black pepper
1 cup dried lima beans,
  cooked

1. Wash the tripe with a combination of lime juice and cold water and cut into small pieces.
2. Bring the water to boil in a saucepan . Add the tripe, garlic, salt and curry powder.
3. Lower heat to medium and simmer until the tripe is tender.
4. Add the onions, scallion, tomato, sliced Scotch bonnet pepper, thyme and black pepper. Add more water if necessary.
5. Reduce heat to low and simmer for 10 minutes, then add the cooked beans. Continue to simmer for a further 5-10 minutes until the liquid is reduced to a desired consistency.

Serve with piping hot cooked rice.
Makes 4 servings.

# COW'S FOOT AND LIMA BEANS

*Cow's foot, also called cow's heel, is usually cleaned and packaged in various quantities and sold in meat shops. However some large meat shops sell them whole. Ask the butcher to cut it up for you.*

1 whole cow's foot, chopped in pieces
8 cups water
1 tablespoon curry powder or paprika, for colouring
1 cup dried lima beans
2 cloves garlic, crushed
1 teaspoon salt
Spinners (optional) see recipe page 24
1 medium onion, coarsely chopped
2 sprigs or ½ teaspoon thyme leaves
1 unbroken Scotch Bonnet pepper

1. Wash the pieces of cow's foot.
2. Bring the water to boil in a large saucepan.
3. Add the cow's foot, curry powder or paprika, crushed garlic and salt. Cover and cook for 1-2 hours or until the pieces are partially cooked.
4. Add the dried beans, spinners, onion, thyme, and unbroken Scotch Bonnet pepper and more water if necessary.
5. Continue to simmer until the beans are tender, the meat is almost separating from the bone and the gravy reaches a desired consistency.

Makes 4 servings.

# SEAFOOD

# SEAFOOD

There are many varieties of fish in Jamaica but the most widely used are goat fish, grouper, kingfish, parrot, snapper, and jackfish. Each time I visit Jamaica, I look forward to my trip to Port Royal or Hellshire Beach in Kingston where fishermen bring their catch. It's quite an experience. Customers are allowed to pick their fish from the fisherman's catch and have it steamed or fried on the spot by local restaurateurs in their little cooking shacks. If your choice is fish tea you would get a whole fish in a broth with okras, cho chos, carrots, seasoned with fresh thyme, scallion and hot pepper, served piping hot. If the fish is fried it is served with bammy or festival.

When buying fish be sure they are fresh — the eyes should be bright, not cloudy, and the gills red. You could also test the freshness by pressing lightly on the meaty side of the fish. If the flesh remains depressed, the fish is not fresh.

King Fish Cutlets...59

Escoveitched Fish...60

Red Snapper in Brown Stew...62

Ina's Quick Baked Fish Fillet...64

Baked or Grilled Snapper with Spinach or Callaloo...65

King Fish Cooked in Coconut Milk...66

Curried Lobster...67

Lobster Creole...68

Curried Shrimp...69

Shrimp Rundown...70

Salted Codfish & Mackerel Dishes...71

# KING FISH CUTLETS

2 lbs King Fish, sliced
   thinly
Limes or lemon juice
Black pepper and salt
   to taste
1 teaspoon paprika
1 cup breadcrumbs
2 eggs lightly stirred
   with a fork to break
   yolks (do not beat)
Oil for frying
Chopped parsley,
   wedges of tomato
   and slices of lemon
   for garnish

1. Wash the fish with plenty of water and lime or lemon juice, dry with paper towels.
2. Sprinkle with salt, paprika, and black pepper.
3. Add a little salt, black pepper and paprika to breadcrumbs.
4. Dip the fish slices in the egg, then in breadcrumbs, coating well, set on paper towels to dry coating.
5. Fry in hot oil until golden brown.
6. Drain on paper towels, place in a oven proof dish and set in a warm oven for just a few minutes until ready to serve.
7. Garnish with parsley, slices of lemon and wedges of tomato.

Makes 2-4 servings

# ESCOVEITCHED FISH

*This style of preparing fish is a traditional Spanish technique encountered through-out Latin America where it is called escabeche. An escabeche is made by pouring a tangy marinade of olive oil, vinegar, onions, and whole allspice over fried fish. Virtually the same dish is highly popular in Jamaica, where it is called 'escoveitch'. Escoveitch fish is traditionally served with bammies, hard dough bread, fried dumplings or festivals.*

*Fish prepared in this manner usually lasts a few days. King Fish, Snapper, Jack, Goatfish, Grunt, Parrot and Sprat are best for this dish, but any other firm fish can be used.*

3 lbs fresh fish
Juice of 2-3 limes or
   lemons to wash fish
1 teaspoon salt
4 teaspoon black
   pepper
Cooking oil for frying
1½ cups vinegar
2 large onions, thinly
   sliced
1 Scotch Bonnet
   pepper cut in thin
   rings
Few dozen pimento
   seeds (whole
   allspice)

1. Clean and wash the fish in water and lime juice.
2. Remove excess water with paper towels.
3. Rub salt and black pepper on both sides and inside the cavity.
4. Place fish on paper towel to dry.
5. In a frying pan, heat a generous amount of oil to boiling point.
6. Fry the fish, a few at a time, on both sides until brown and slightly crisp.
7. Arrange them on a large platter or in a deep bowl.
8. Remove the pan from the heat, set aside to cool, drain and discard the oil.
9. Lower heat and return the frying pan. Pour in the vinegar and add the onions, peppers and pimento seeds.

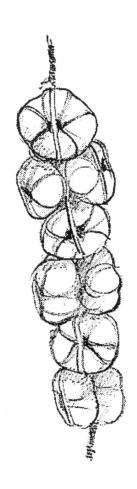

10. Simmer over a low heat until the onions are tender (vinegar evaporates rapidly if the heat is too high).
11. Remove from the heat and set aside to cool.
12. Pour the mixture over the fish and leave to marinate overnight or until ready to serve.

Makes 4-6 servings.

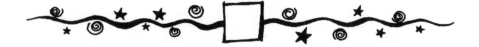

# RED SNAPPER IN BROWN STEW

*This is my favourite way of cooking red snapper, and the inspiration for writing this cookbook. It is said that fish retains its juice when cooked with the head and tail intact.*

3 Snappers, medium sized
Lime juice
1 teaspoon salt
½ teaspoon black pepper
Flour
Cooking oil for frying
1½ cups water
1 onion, thinly sliced
1 large tomato, coarsely chopped
1 dozen pimento seeds (whole allspice)
2 sprigs or 1 teaspoon thyme leaves
1 tablespoon butter
4 slices Scotch bonnet pepper, seeds removed

1. Clean and wash the fish with lime juice and water.
2. Dry with paper towels.
3. Make one diagonal cut on each side of the fish.
4. Rub salt and black pepper into the cavity and incisions.
5. Heat a generous amount of oil in a frying pan until it's very hot.
6. Coat the fish with flour to prevent them sticking to the pan.
7. Place them in the hot oil, one at a time, leaving a little space between to prevent them sticking together.
8. Fry on both sides until they are golden brown. Remove from the pan and set aside.
9. Remove the frying pan from heat, allow to cool and drain off the oil.
10. Pour 1½ cups water in the frying pan.
11. Add the onions, tomato, pimento seeds, thyme, butter and pieces of Scotch Bonnet pepper.

12. Return the pan to the stove and bring to a boil.
13. Add the fish, cover and simmer for 10 minutes or until the sauce is reduced to desired thickness.
14. Taste, add salt and black pepper if needed.

Serve with steaming rice and peas, or green bananas, yams and fresh green salad.

Makes 3-4 servings

# INA'S QUICK BAKED FISH FILLET

*This recipe comes from Ina, one of my sisters living in Jamaica.*

1½ lbs fish fillet

Lime

½ teaspoon salt

¼ teaspoon black
   pepper

½ teaspoon dry
   mustard

½ cup cow's milk

1½ teaspoons
   Worcestershire
   sauce

2½ cups bread crumbs

3 tablespoons melted
   butter

1. Wash the fish in lime and water.
2. Dry on paper towels and set aside.
3. Mix together the salt, pepper, dry mustard, Worcestershire sauce and milk.
4. Dip the fish fillets into the milk mixture, then into the bread crumbs.
5. Place the fish in a greased shallow baking dish and brush with melted butter.
6. Bake in preheated oven at 450° F for 15-20 minutes until flaked and moist.

Makes 2-4 servings

# BAKED OR GRILLED SNAPPER STUFFED WITH SPINACH OR CALLALOO

*This makes an excellent dish for a summer brunch.*

2 medium sized red
   snappers or jackfish
   can also be used
Lime
1 teaspoon allspice
½ teaspoon salt
1 teaspoon black
   pepper
1 tablespoon margarine

**Stuffing**

½ lb spinach or callaloo,
   finely chopped
1 small onion, finely
   chopped
1 teaspoon fresh
   thyme, minced
Few pieces of hot
   pepper, finely
   chopped
Dash of black pepper
   and salt

1. Clean the fish thoroughly and wash with lime and water.
2. Dry the fish with paper towels. Make slits on both sides.
3. Combine the allspice, salt and black pepper and rub the mixture all over the fish and inside cavity. Set aside on paper towels.
4. Use a knife to spread approximately 1 tablespoon margarine inside the cavity and all over each fish.
5. Combine all the ingredients for the stuffing and fill the cavities of each fish with the mixture. Secure with cocktail picks.
6. Wrap each fish in aluminum foil.
7. Bake in preheated oven at 350° F, or on the barbeque grill for, 40-45 minutes or until fish flakes easily when tested with a fork.

NOTE: When serving remove cocktail picks.

Makes 2 servings

# KING FISH COOKED IN COCONUT MILK

*Salmon steaks are also absolutely delicious when cooked in this manner.*

1 lb kingfish steaks
Lime
½ teaspoon black
 pepper
¼ teaspoon salt
½ cup cooking oil
2 cups concentrated
 coconut milk (see
 recipe page 74)
1 onion, sliced in thin
 rings
1 tomato, sliced in
 small rings
½ teaspoon paprika (for
 colouring)
1 sprig thyme, minced
1 whole Scotch Bonnet
 pepper

1. Wash the fish steaks in lime and water and pat dry.
2. Sprinkle salt and black pepper on both sides, set aside.
3. Heat the oil in a frying pan and fry the fish steaks until brown on both sides. Remove from pan and set aside.
4. Boil the coconut milk in a saucepan until the liquid is reduced to a combination of oil and custard.
5. Place the fish steaks, onion, tomato, paprika, thyme and the whole Scotch Bonnet pepper in the saucepan with the coconut. Simmer until the onion is tender and the fish flakes easily when tested with a fork. Be careful not to allow the custard to burn.
6. Taste for flavour and add salt and black pepper if necessary.

Makes 2 servings

# CURRIED LOBSTER

*In Jamaica the spawning period for lobsters is between April and June. During that time hunting them is prohibited to allow them to regenerate. Lobster dishes are not often served in Jamaican households because the fishermen's catch is usually sold to meet the demand of establishments catering for tourists.*

¼ cup margarine

2 large onions, sliced thinly

1 clove garlic, minced

3 tablespoons curry power

3 tomatoes, coarsely chopped

1 green sweet pepper, sliced in rings

1 sprig thyme, fresh or dried

1 Scotch Bonnet pepper, chopped (remove seeds)

1 cup water

Salt and black pepper to taste

2 cups lobster meat

1. Heat the margarine in a deep skillet. Add the onions and garlic and sauté.
2. Add the curry powder and stir for 1 or 2 minutes.
3. Stir in the tomatoes, green sweet pepper, thyme, Scotch Bonnet pepper and water.
4. Bring the mixture to a boil, reduce heat.
5. Gently stir in the lobster meat, being careful not to break up the chunks.
6. Add black pepper and salt to taste.
7. Simmer for 10 minutes or until the liquid is reduced to desired consistency.

Serve with steaming boiled rice and a fresh salad or cooked vegetables.

Makes 6 servings

# LOBSTER CREOLE

1 onion, coarsely
  chopped
2 sweet peppers, sliced
  in rings (seeds
  removed)
4 tablespoon cooking
  oil
1 tomato, coarsely
  chopped
2 lbs cooked and
  shredded lobster
  meat
Salt and pepper to
  taste
2 tablespoon rum or
  sherry (optional)

1. Sauté the onion and peppers in oil until tender.
2. Add the tomato, lobster meat, salt and pepper. Simmer for 5 minutes.
3. Add the rum or sherry. Continue to simmer for another 10 minutes or until tender and about ⅔ of the liquid is absorbed.

Serve with plain boiled rice, cooked vegetables or fresh salad.

Makes 4-6 servings.

# CURRIED SHRIMP

2 lbs cooked shrimps (or raw shrimps shelled and deveined)
3 tablespoons margarine
1 onion, sliced in thin rings
2 Irish (white) potatoes peeled and diced
1 clove garlic, crushed
1 Scotch Bonnet pepper, minced(seeds removed)
1½ tablespoons curry powder
¼ cup flour
1 cup water
Salt and black pepper to taste

1. Heat the margarine in a skillet and sauté the onion, potato, garlic, and Scotch Bonnet pepper.
2. Mix the curry and flour in the water. Gradually add the mixture to the sautéed ingredients.
3. Add salt and black pepper, stirring and gradually bringing to a boil.
4. Reduce heat and simmer uncovered for 20 minutes.
5. Add the shrimps, cover and simmer gently for another 10 minutes.
6. Taste for salt and add if necessary.

Serve hot on a bed of fluffy cooked rice with steamed vegetables or a fresh salad. Makes 4-6 servings.

# SHRIMP RUNDOWN

1 lb large frozen or
   fresh shrimp
Lime
1 cup concentrated
   coconut milk (see
   recipe page 74)
1 small onion, coarsely
   chopped
1 tomato, coarsely
   chopped
¼ teaspoon black
   pepper
1 sprig fresh thyme
¼ teaspoon salt
¼ teaspoon paprika or
   annato (for
   colouring)
Few pieces of Scotch
   Bonnet pepper

1. Thaw the shrimps if frozen, and wash with lime water and set aside.
2. Bring the coconut milk to boil in a saucepan.
3. Add the onion, tomato, paprika, pieces of pepper, thyme and salt.
4. Simmer until the onions are tender and the mixture is slightly thickened, about 10 minutes.
5. Add shrimps and simmer gently for about 2 to 5 minutes.
6. Taste for flavour and add more salt and black pepper, if necessary.

Serve with boiled green bananas or on a bed of cooked rice with a carrot salad or tossed salad.

Makes 4 servings.

# SALTED CODFISH & MACKEREL DISHES

Pickled fish was introduced to the slaves by the European slave masters, although fresh fish was in abundance. Evidently, the slaves acquired the taste for salted meats and fish which they passed down from generation to generation. Today salted fish continues to play an important part in West Indian cuisine.

Ackee and Salted Codfish..72

Rundown..73

Coconut Milk..74

Codfish and Broccoli..75

Codfish and Callaloo..75

Ina's Mackerel and Green Banana Casserole..76

Salted Codfish Salad..77

# ACKEE AND SALTED CODFISH

*Jamaicans are just about the only people in the world to eat ackee and we like it so much that ackee with salted codfish is one of the national dishes. It was brought to the island during the slave trade and now is exported in cans and is available in Jamaican and other West Indian food stores. Ackee is a red pod fruit that eventually opens to show off the yellow edible portion. The unripe ackees contain a highly toxic substance and can be deadly if eaten before they are mature. When cooked, some say it reminds them of scrambled eggs!*

*Fried dumplings, boiled green bananas, yams, or cooked rice are a splendid complement to this dish.*

½ lb salted codfish
2 cans ackee, drained
½ cup cooking oil
1 medium-sized onion, finely chopped
1 medium sized tomato, chopped in small pieces
Few pieces of hot peppers (seeds removed)
6 strips bacon, fried crisp (optional)
Black pepper
¼ teaspoon thyme leaves

1. Cook the codfish in water for 15 minutes, discard water.
2. Rinse the fish in cold water so that you can remove the bones and skin without burning your fingers. Flake and set aside.
3. Wash the ackee in a colander with hot water to remove the brine, set aside.
4. Heat the oil in a frying pan.
5. Add the onions, tomato, hot pepper and thyme. Sauté until the onions are tender.
6. Add the ackee and fish and mix gently together.
7. Sprinkle with black pepper.
8. Lay the crispy fried bacon strips on top.

Serve hot.
Makes 4-6 servings.

# RUNDOWN

*"Run Down" is the Jamaican method of reducing coconut milk slowly to make a combination of oil and custard. Salted mackerel or salted codfish are added towards the end of the reducing process. Traditionally, it is served with boiled green bananas, flour dumplings and roasted or boiled breadfruit, when in season. Fresh limeade is a perfect beverage with this dish.*

2 whole pickled mackerel
2 cups concentrated coconut milk (see below)
1 large onion, sliced in thin rings
1 unbroken Scotch Bonnet pepper
1 large tomato, coarsely chopped
2 sprigs or ½ teaspoon dried thyme leaves
¼ teaspoon black pepper

1. Soak the mackerel for 6 hours, or overnight, in cold water to remove excess salt. Pour off cold water.
2. Add boiling water and soak for a further 2 minutes. Pour off water and cool.
3. Remove fins, bones and heads. Cut fish in fairly large pieces and set aside.
4. Boil the coconut milk until it separates into a combination of thick sauce and oil.
5. Add the mackerel, onion, unbroken pepper, tomato, thyme and black pepper.
6. Simmer for 10 minutes, stirring occasionally. Do not allow the sauce to burn as it thickens.
7. Remove whole pepper.

Serve with boiled green bananas.
Makes 4-6 servings

# COCONUT MILK

*Only use coconuts that have water inside; you should hear the water moving if you shake the coconut. To remove the shell, hold the coconut in the palm of the hand and crack the shell in several places with a hammer. Hold the coconut over a container to catch the water. Drink the water or discard. If the shell is not completely detached use a dull flat kitchen knife and work it between the meat and shell until the meat separates from the shell.*

2 coconuts
2 cups warm water

**Method 1:**
1. Grate the coconut into a bowl.
2. Add the warm water to the grated coconut and squeeze by hand to extract all of the milk.
3. Strain the liquid through a fine sieve or cheesecloth, discard thrash.

OR

**Method 2:**
1. Cut the coconut into very small pieces. Put 2 handfuls at a time with enough water to cover in a food processor fitted with a steel blade.
2. Adjust to grate for 15-20 seconds or until the pieces resemble grated carrots.
3. Strain the liquid through a sieve. Add more water for a thinner milk.

# CODFISH AND BROCCOLI

*This one's from my mother. This dish is traditionally made with Jamaica's famous vegetable — callaloo, and served for breakfast, with boiled green bananas or fried dumplings. I was delighted to find that broccoli could make such a delicious substitute for callaloo!*

½ lb codfish

1 bunch broccoli, florets separated from main stalk, each floret cut in 2

1 tomato, coarsely chopped

½ cup cooking oil

1 small onion, finely chopped

¼ teaspoon fresh thyme leaves

Black pepper to taste

1. Place codfish in saucepan with enough water to cover. Boil for 15 minutes.
2. Remove from heat. Drain, set side to cool and remove skin and bones.
3. Steam broccoli in a minimum amount of water for approximately 3 minutes, do not overcook.
4. Remove from heat, discard water and set aside.
5. Heat oil in a skillet, add the onion and tomato and sauté until the onion is tender.
6. Combine the broccoli, salted fish and seasonings in the skillet.
7. Sprinkle with thyme and black pepper and simmer for 5 minutes.

Serve with fried dumplings or bread.
Makes 6 servings

## CODFISH AND CALLALOO

*Prepare in the same manner as above but use callaloo instead of broccoli. Clean, wash and finely chop the callaloo.*

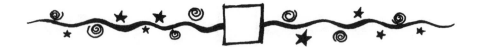

# INA'S MACKEREL AND GREEN BANANA CASSEROLE

*This is a splendid dish for Sunday brunch!*
*Salted mackerel fillet is perfect because there are no heads or bones.*

1 dozen green bananas
1 cup cow's milk
2 lbs salted mackerel
  (soak overnight to
  remove excess salt)
½ lb carrots, diced
2 cups concentrated
  coconut milk
1 medium sized tomato
1 medium sized onion,
  sliced in thin rings
Black pepper to taste
Margarine

1. In a pot bring to the boil enough water to cover the bananas.
2. Score the bananas lengthwise, leave the skins on. Boil for 20 minutes or until the skin easily separates from the bananas.
3. When cooked, remove the skin.
4. Add the cow's milk to the bananas and mash until fluffy. Set aside.
5. Drain the water from the mackerels and scald with boiling water. Discard water. If whole mackerel is used remove the heads and bones.
6. Flake and set aside.
7. Cook the carrots in the coconut milk until the milk thickens to a sauce.
8. Add the chopped tomato, onion and black pepper and simmer until the onion is tender.
9. Add the mackerel and combine.
10. Line a casserole dish with half of the creamed bananas.
11. Pour in the mackerel mixture and cover with the remaining creamed bananas.
12. Brush with margarine.
13. Cover dish and reheat in oven for 5 minutes.

Serve hot.
Makes 6 servings

# SALTED CODFISH SALAD

*This salad varies throughout the Caribbean, known as Brule Jol in St. Lucia and in Trinidad & Tobago as Buljol.*

½ lb salted, uncooked codfish
1 cucumber, peeled and sliced
2 tomatoes, coarsely chopped
2 tablespoons vinegar or lime juice
3 tablespoons salad oil
1 Scotch bonnet pepper, sliced (seeds removed)
Dash of black pepper

1. To remove excess salt, soak fish in plenty of water for at least 2 hours.
2. Remove skin and bones, flake fish.
3. Place in bowl and add the cucumber, tomatoes, vinegar or lime juice and hot pepper.
4. Mix well, adjust the seasonings to taste.

Serve with unsalted crackers or hard dough bread.

# EASY ON THE BUDGET BUT NUTRITIOUS

# EASY ON THE BUDGET BUT NUTRITIOUS

Here are a few simple dishes which can be made at a short notice, using the ingredients in your "pantry". Some of these ingredients are usually put away for the "leany days".

Seasoned Rice with Salted Codfish...81

Stewed Salted Codfish with Cho Cho...82

Corned Beef and Cabbage...83

Tinned Fresh Herrings or Sardines..84

Stewed Peas and Rice...85

# SEASONED RICE WITH SALTED CODFISH

1 lb salted codfish
¼ cup cooking oil
1 onion, sliced thinly
2 small tomatoes,
   coarsely chopped
Few pieces of hot
   pepper
1 sprig thyme
3 cups water
2 cups rice, washed

1. Boil the fish for approximately 15 minutes.
2. Run under cold water, remove skin and bones and shred fish.
3. Heat the oil in a saucepan add the onions and sauté.
4. Add the fish, tomatoes, pieces of hot pepper and thyme.
5. Add the water then stir in the rice.
6. Cover the saucepan and bring to boil.
7. Lower heat to medium and simmer for 20 minutes or until the rice is tender.
8. Serve with slices of avocado pear.

Makes 2-4 servings

# STEWED SALTED CODFISH WITH CHO CHO

*This dish is delicious, economical, and versatile. Lima beans, pumpkin or carrots can be added to make an excellent variety. Carrots and pumpkin add colour and contrast to dish.*

½ lb saltfish

2 cups concentrated coconut milk (see recipe page 74)

2 cho chos, peeled and sliced

1 onion, sliced thinly

1 sprig thyme

¼ teaspoon paprika or annato (to colour)

1 tablespoon flour

¼ cup water

Black pepper to taste

1. Soak fish in cold water for at least 2 hours, or boil for 15 minutes. Drain and cool for easy handling.
2. Remove the skin, and bones. Flake fish and set aside.
3. Bring the coconut milk to a boil in a saucepan. Add the cho cho, onion, thyme, paprika and flaked fish.
4. Simmer until the cho cho and onion are tender.
5. Mix flour and water.
6. Blend the flour mixture with the other ingredients until the sauce thickens.
7. Add more water if the sauce gets too thick.
8. Sprinkle with black pepper.
9. Stir and simmer for another 5 minutes.

Serve on a bed of cooked rice, garnish with fresh parsley.

Makes 2-4 servings

NOTE: Sauce consistency should be similar to cheese sauce

# CORNED BEEF AND CABBAGE

*Jamaicans call this dish "Bully Beef and Cabbage".*

1 tablespoon cooking oil

1 small cabbage, shredded

1 onion, thinly sliced

1 medium tomato, coarsely chopped

¼ cup water

1 tin corned beef (bully beef)

¼ teaspoon thyme leaves

Dash of black pepper

1. Heat oil in a saucepan. Add the cabbage, onion, and tomato and sauté until the cabbage is limp.
2. Add water, cover and simmer for 5 minutes.
3. Add the corned beef and stir until it integrates with the vegetables.
4. Sprinkle with thyme and black pepper. Simmer for another 5 minutes.

Serve on a bed of plain boiled rice.

Makes 4 servings.

# TINNED FRESH HERRINGS OR SARDINES

*This is another simple but very nutritious dish. Sardines provide a very high source of calcium.*

1 tablespoon cooking oil

Few pieces of hot pepper

1 tomato, coarsely chopped

1 tin fresh herrings or 2 tins sardines

1 small onion, sliced thinly

1 cup rice, cooked

1. Heat the oil and sauté the onion, pepper, and tomato in a saucepan.
2. Add the herrings or sardines (including the sauce) and simmer for 5 minutes.
3. Sprinkle with black pepper.

Serve on a bed of piping hot cooked rice.
Makes 2-3 servings.

# STEWED PEAS AND RICE

1 lb pig's tail or salt
   beef, cut into
   serving-sized pieces
1 lb stewing beef
10 cups water
2 cups dried red peas
   (kidney beans)
2 cloves garlic, crushed
Spinners (recipe page
   24)
1 onion, thinly sliced
1 stalk scallion,
   crushed
2 sprigs thyme
1 unbroken Scotch
   Bonnet Pepper
Black pepper

1. Soak pig's tail or salt beef in cold water
   overnight then discard water.
2. Pour the 10 cups of water in a large pot,
   bring to the boil and add the pig's tail or
   salt beef, stewing beef, peas and crushed
   garlic.
3. Bring to a boil, cover the pot and simmer
   until the meats and peas are tender.
4. Add the spinners, onion, scallion, thyme,
   unbroken hot pepper and black pepper to
   taste, add more water if necessary.
5. Stir, cover and simmer for another 15
   minutes. The stew should be fairly thick
   and peas almost disintegrating. No addi-
   tional thickening is necessary. The stew
   consistency should be similar to chili con
   carne. If stew is not thick enough increase
   heat and simmer for a few minutes being
   careful not to boil too much or the peas
   will burn.

Serve hot on a bed of plain cooked rice.
Makes 4-6 servings

# VEGETABLES, LEGUMES & SALADS

# VEGETARIAN

Although I am an avid meat eater, vegetables also play an important part of my diet. Some days, when meat was scarce in our home, my mom would prepare a meatless dish that was so delicious we hardly noticed the absence of meat. It's of interest to note that although most Jamaicans are carnivorous some of the natives, such as the Rastafarians do not eat meat because of their religious beliefs. Some of the recipes were passed on to me by friends and some were reconstructed from old memories. I have tested, tried and adjusted the ingredients to be consistent with the Jamaican flavour.

Vegetable Patties...89

Pumpkin Fritters...91

Cornmeal Fritters...92

Spinach Omelette...93

Green Banana Pancake...95

Okra with Eggs...96

Eggplant Topped with Scrambled Eggs and Tomatoes...97

Hearty Vegetable Soup...98

Lentils & Rice...100

Stewed Ackees with Tomatoes...101

Callaloo & Rice Cook-up...102

Curried Cabbage with or without Salted Codfish...103

Ackee, Rice & Cheese Casserole...104

Rundown Ital Style...105

Steamed Mixed Vegetables...106

# VEGETABLE PATTIES

**Pastry**

2 cups flour

½ teaspoon salt
(optional)

½ cup vegetable oil

Iced water

**Filling**

1½ cups mixed
vegetables - corn,
carrots, sweet peas
and string beans

¼ teaspoon salt
(optional)

2 tablespoons
vegetable oil

1 medium-sized onion
finely chopped

2 stalks scallion or
green onion, finely
minced

½ Scotch bonnet pepper
minced, seeds
removed

½ tablespoon curry
powder(optional

½ teaspoon thyme
leaves

**Pastry**

1. Combine the flour and salt in a bowl and
   stir in the vegetable oil.
2. When the mixture resembles bread
   crumbs add the iced water, a little at a
   time, until a dough is formed.
3. Using your hands, shape the dough into
   a ball, wrap it in aluminum foil and
   refrigerate for 15-20 minutes.
4. In the meantime prepare filling for patties.

**Filling**

*I use the frozen mixed vegetables because the prepa-
ration is less time consuming. Frozen vegetables
retain just as many minerals and vitamins as the
fresh ones.*

1. Cook the vegetables until tender but not
   overcooked (add a little salt if needed),
   pour into a colander to drain.
2. Heat the vegetable oil in a skillet and
   sauté the onion, scallion and pieces of
   pepper, add the curry powder and stir,
   add the mixed vegetables and thyme,
   stir.
3. Cover and simmer for 1 minute. Remove
   from heat and set aside to cool.

**Patty Casings**

1. Separate the dough into 12 equal pieces and sprinkle with flour.
2. Roll out the dough. Using a knife or cookie cutter, cut around an upside down saucer to make an even circle.
3. Place enough filling on one side of each circle. Fold the other half over and seal the edges by crimping them with a fork.
4. Bake the patties on ungreased baking sheets in a preheated oven at 400° F for 20 minutes.

Makes 12-14 patties

# PUMPKIN FRITTERS

1 lb fresh pumpkin
4 tablespoons sugar
1 tablespoon butter or
  margarine
2 eggs
5 tablespoons flour
½ cup cooking oil

1. Peel the pumpkin and cut in into 1″ pieces.
2. Place the pieces in a pot with water to cover and cook until tender.
3. Remove from the heat and pour off water.
4. Crush the cooked pumpkin in a bowl.
5. Stir in sugar, butter and eggs.
6. Add the flour slowly and keep stirring.
7. Heat the oil in a frying pan. Drop 1 tablespoonful of the mixture at a time into the hot oil until the pan is full. Space fritters apart. Fry on both sides until golden brown.
8. Remove fritters from the pan and place on paper towels to absorb excess oil.

Makes 4-6 servings

# CORNMEAL FRITTERS

¼ cup cornmeal
¼ cup flour
½ teaspoon baking powder
¼ teaspoon salt
½ cup cow's milk or coconut milk
1 small onion, finely chopped
½ hot pepper, finely chopped, deseeded
½ teaspoon fresh thyme
Vegetable oil for frying

1. Mix together the cornmeal, flour, baking power and salt in a bowl.
2. Slowly stir in the milk until the mixture is smooth.
3. Stir in the onion, pepper and thyme.
4. Heat the vegetable oil in a frying pan and drop tablespoons of the mixture into the heated oil.
5. Fry until one side is golden then turn over and fry the other side.

Best when served warm
Makes 4 servings

# SPINACH OMELETTE

*Callaloo can be used instead of spinach.*

1 lb fresh or frozen leaf
spinach
4 tablespoons butter or
margarine
1 small onion, finely
minced
½ teaspoon salt
¼ teaspoon black
pepper
6 eggs, beaten

1. Wash spinach thoroughly and drain. Place in a saucepan with ½ cup water and cook over moderate heat until tender. Pour into a colander to drain water. Chop coarsely.
2. Melt ½ tablespoon of the butter or margarine in a saucepan, add the onion and sauté until tender. Add the salt, black pepper and spinach, stirring well. Set aside and keep hot.
3. Melt 2 tablespoons of the butter or margarine in a frying pan, beat 3 of the eggs, pour into the pan and cook over a low heat until just set.
4. Place half of the spinach mixture on top of the eggs carefully spreading it evenly over them. Cook for about 5 minutes.
5. Place a large plate over the frying pan and carefully turn the omelette upside down on to the plate.
6. Melt the remaining butter or margarine in the frying pan and pour in the remaining 3 beaten eggs. When the eggs are cooked, spread the remaining spinach over the top and cook for about 5 minutes.

7. Carefully slide the first omelette back into the pan on top of the other one.
8. Cook for a further 2-3 minutes to heat through and then slide the whole omelette on to a serving plate. Cut into wedges and serve.

Bread or boiled potatoes are delicious with this dish.
Makes 2-4 servings

# GREEN BANANA PANCAKE

4 green bananas
  peeled
½ cup water
1 medium-sized onion,
  finely chopped
½ teaspoon salt
  (optional)
1 tablespoon flour
½ teaspoon freshly
  grated nutmeg
3 tablespoons
  vegetable oil

1. Place the peeled bananas in a food processor and blend until smooth, adding the water a little at a time to produce a smooth consistency.
2. Pour the banana mixture in a bowl. Add the finely chopped onion, salt, flour and nutmeg, combine all the ingredients.
3. Heat the vegetable oil in a frying pan, pour in the banana mixture and fry on both sides until golden brown.

Cut in wedges and serve garnished with a salad.
Makes 4 servings

# OKRA WITH EGGS

1 lb small okras

2 tablespoons lemon juice

4 tablespoons butter or margarine

1 small onion, thinly sliced

1 small sweet red pepper, thinly sliced

2 large tomatoes, chopped

3 eggs

Salt to taste

¼ teaspoon black pepper

1 teaspoon thyme leaves

1. Rinse the okras and trim the stems, taking care not to cut into the okras.
2. Half-fill a large saucepan with water and bring to the boil.
3. Add the okra and lemon juice and simmer for 5 minutes. Drain.
4. Melt half the butter in a large frying pan, add the onion and red sweet pepper, fry until the vegetables are tender.
5. Lay the okra over the onion and pepper, sprinkle the chopped tomatoes over the top.
6. Melt the remaining butter and pour it over the vegetables. Cover the pan and simmer for about 10 minutes, or until the okras are tender.
7. In a bowl beat the eggs with the salt, black pepper and thyme.
8. Pour the egg mixture slowly over the vegetables and continue to cook until the eggs are set. Serve immediately.

Makes 2-3 servings

# EGGPLANT TOPPED WITH SCRAMBLED EGGS AND TOMATOES

4 medium-sized
  eggplants
2 tablespoons butter or
  vegetable oil
1 medium-sized onion,
  chopped
2 large cloves garlic,
  crushed
1 red pepper (sweet
  pepper) thinly sliced,
  seeds removed
4 large tomatoes
  chopped
6 eggs
Salt to taste
½ teaspoon black
  pepper

1. Make 2 or 3 slits in each eggplant with a sharp knife and place in a 450° F oven.
2. When the skins are black and the flesh soft when poked with a finger, remove and set aside to cool. Peel and discard skin.
3. Place the pulp in a bowl and mash with a fork. Arrange in a shallow dish and keep warm.
4. Melt the butter in a large frying pan, add the onion, crushed garlic and pepper and sauté until the vegetables are tender. Add the tomatoes and sauté for another 5 minutes, stirring frequently.
5. Beat the eggs, salt and black pepper in a bowl and pour into the frying pan with the sautéed vegetables. Stir well then leave over a low heat for a few minutes until the eggs are set.
6. Spoon the mixture over the eggplants and serve immediately.

Serve with bread.
Makes 2-4 servings

# HEARTY VEGETABLE SOUP

1 lb yam, peeled, washed and cut in chunks
½ lb sweet potatoes, peeled, washed and cut in chunks
2 medium-sized Irish (white) potatoes, peeled, washed and cut in chunks
2 large carrots, scraped, washed and sliced
1 cho cho, peeled, washed and cut into quarters
1 lb pumpkin, peeled, washed, seeds removed and diced
2 large cloves garlic
12 cups water
2 cups coconut milk
1 lb callaloo or spinach, washed, thick stems removed and chopped
1 small cabbage, washed and coarsely chopped
1 medium-sized onion
2 stalks scallion or green onion
2 sprigs thyme
1 whole Scotch Bonnet pepper
Fresh ground black pepper to taste
Salt (optional)

1. Place the yam, potatoes, carrots, cho cho, pumpkin and garlic in a large saucepan with 12 cups water, bring to boil and simmer on medium heat for 10 minutes.
2. Add the coconut milk, callaloo, cabbage, onion, scallion, thyme and whole Scotch Bonnet pepper. Add more water if necessary (the liquid should be at least 2 inches above the ingredients).
3. Stir and simmer for another 15 minutes or until the vegetables are soft and the soup reaches a desired consistency. Sprinkle with black pepper, salt to taste. Remove the whole pepper before serving.

# PUMPKIN WITH RICE

1 cup long-grain rice, washed thoroughly

3 cups water

1 lb pumpkin, peeled, washed, seeds removed and diced

½ teaspoon salt (optional)

1 small onion, thinly sliced

1 sprig thyme

1 tablespoon butter or vegetable oil

1. Place the rice in a saucepan with the water and bring to the boil.
2. Add the pumpkin, salt, sliced onion, thyme and butter, and stir. Bring to a boil, reduce heat to medium and simmer for 15-20 minutes until the pumpkin and rice are soft and the water is absorbed.

Garnish with sliced avocado.

Makes 2-4 servings

# LENTILS AND RICE

1 cup brown lentils,
    washed and drained
3 cups water
½ cup vegetable oil
2 large onions, thinly
    sliced
Salt to taste (optional)
½ teaspoon black
    pepper
1 cup boiling water
1 cup long-grain rice,
    washed thoroughly
    and drained

1. Put the lentils into a large saucepan, cover with the 3 cups water and bring to the boil. Lower the heat, cover and cook for 25-30 minutes or until the lentils are almost cooked and the water is almost absorbed.

2. Heat the oil in a frying pan, add the sliced onions and sauté, stirring frequently until they are dark golden, but not burnt. Reserve half of the onions and the oil; stir the other half into the lentils.

3. Add the salt, black pepper and 1 cup boiling water and bring to the boil. Stir in the rice and bring to the boil.

4. Lower the heat, cover and simmer for a further 15-20 minutes, or until the lentils and rice are tender and the water absorbed.

5. Remove from the heat and leave to stand for 10-15 minutes.

6. Pile on to a plate and garnish with the remaining onions and oil.

Makes 4-6 Servings

# STEWED ACKEES WITH TOMATOES

*The colour of this dish is a beautiful contrast of red and yellow and the taste is absolutely delicious!*

2 tablespoons
vegetable oil
1 medium-sized onion,
sliced in thin rings
1 clove garlic, minced
1 cup or 3 small
tomatoes, coarsely
chopped
3 whole cloves
1 whole Scotch Bonnet
pepper
1 can ackees
¼ teaspoon salt or juice
of ½ lime
¼ teaspoon freshly
ground black pepper
Dash of Pickapeppa or
Tabasco sauce
(optional)

1. Heat the vegetable oil in a frying pan and sauté the onion and garlic until tender. Add the chopped tomatoes, cloves and whole Scotch Bonnet pepper. Simmer until the mixture has cooked to a thickish sauce.
2. Pour the ackee in a colander and rinse with very hot water to remove the brine, drain thoroughly.
3. Add the ackee, salt or lime juice to the pan and sprinkle with ground black pepper.
4. Stir gently and simmer for approximately 10 minutes. Remove the whole pepper and discard. Taste and adjust seasoning if required.

Serve hot on a bed of plain cooked rice.
Makes 4 servings.

Ackee

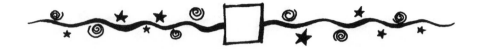

# CALLALOO AND RICE COOK-UP

1 lb salted codfish
  (optional)
1½ teaspoons
  margarine or butter
2 small tomatoes,
  coarsely chopped
1 whole sweet green
  pepper chopped,
  seeds removed
1 stalk scallion,
  chopped
1 sprig or ½ teaspoon
  thyme leaves
1 onion, thinly sliced
1 clove garlic, crushed
12 okras, trimmed,
  washed and sliced
  into rings
1 lb callaloo
2 tablespoons water
2 cups cooked rice
½ teaspoon black
  pepper

1. Boil salted codfish for about 10 minutes occasionally draining and discarding the salted water and adding more water until most of the saltiness is eliminated.  Shred the fish and set aside.
2. Melt the margarine or butter in a saucepan and sauté the tomatoes, green pepper, scallion, thyme, onion and garlic.
3. Add the okras, callaloo and 2 tablespoons water. Cover and steam until tender.
4. Add the cooked rice, salted codfish and black pepper. Stir to combine all the ingredients.

Serve hot.
Make 4-6 servings

# CURRIED CABBAGE WITH OR WITHOUT SALTED CODFISH

2 tablespoons butter or
vegetable oil

1 large onion, coarsely
chopped

½ Scotch Bonnet
pepper, minced,
seeds removed

1½ tablespoons curry
powder

1¼ cups water

2 cups cabbage,
coarsely chopped
and washed

2 sprigs or ½ teaspoon
thyme leaves

1 cup cooked codfish,
deboned and
shredded (optional)

1. Melt the margarine or butter in a
saucepan then add the onion, Scotch
Bonnet pepper and curry powder.
2. Sauté until the onion is tender.
3. Add the cabbage and water, simmer
until tender but not soggy. Add the salted codfish and toss lightly.

Serve on a platter with cooked rice or
boiled green bananas garnish with
tomato slices.
Makes 4 servings

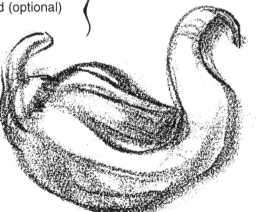

# ACKEE RICE AND CHEESE CASSEROLE

2 cups rice, washed
2 tablespoons butter
1 onion, grated
1 tablespoon flour
1½ cups milk
2 cans ackee, well
    drained
2 cups grated cheese

1. Cook the rice in 4 cups water until tender.
2. Melt butter in a saucepan, add the grated onion and stir.
3. Mix the flour with the milk, making sure there are no lumps.
4. Pour the flour mixture into the saucepan with the grated onion. Stir until smooth.
5. Place a layer of rice in a buttered baking dish, then a layer of the ackee. Spread 2 tablespoons of the onion sauce over the ackee, then a layer of ½ the grated cheese.
6. Repeat the layers of rice, ackee, onion sauce, and cheese.
7. Bake in the oven at 350° F for 30 minutes.

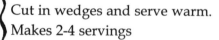

Cut in wedges and serve warm.
Makes 2-4 servings

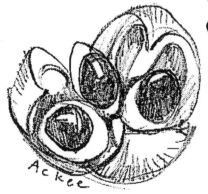

Ackee

# RUNDOWN ITAL STYLE

*The Rastafarians refer to their food as "Ital". It is strictly vegetarian and uses no salt. I have included salt in this recipe as an option.*

**Rundown Sauce**
3 cups concentrated coconut milk (see recipe page 74)
1 medium-sized onion, sliced in rings
1 large clove garlic, minced
2 sprigs or ½ teaspoon thyme leaves
1 sprig parsley
½ teaspoon salt (optional)
2 cloves
Few pieces of Scotch Bonnet pepper
2 thin slices fresh ginger

**Vegetables**
1 teaspoon margarine
2 large carrots, scraped, washed and sliced into small rings
½ cabbage, washed and finely chopped
1 sweet pepper, seeded and chopped
2 whole corn-on-the-cob, cut into six rounds each
Black pepper

### The Sauce
1. Pour the coconut milk into a saucepan and bring to the boil. Add the onion, garlic, thyme, parsley, salt, cloves, pieces of pepper and ginger.
2. Reduce heat to medium and simmer, stirring occasionally until sauce is slightly thick. Remove from heat and set aside.

### The Vegetables
1. Melt the margarine in a large saucepan. Add the vegetables and sauté slightly.
2. Add a little water, cover and cook for about 10 minutes over medium heat.
3. Add the rundown sauce and combine with the vegetables. Reduce heat and simmer for another 2 minutes.

Sprinkle with black pepper and serve immediately.
Makes 2 servings

# STEAMED MIXED VEGETABLES

Vegetable oil

1 large onion coarsely chopped

1 stalk scallion or green onion, minced

1 clove garlic, crushed

1 teaspoon fresh thyme leaves

1 hot pepper, deseeded and finely chopped

1 medium cho cho, peeled, washed, thinly sliced

½ cabbage, washed and cut in small chunks

2 large carrots, scraped, washed, sliced in rings

3 stalks bok choy, or Chinese greens, washed and coarsely chopped

½ teaspoon salt (optional)

Water

1. Heat the vegetable oil in a large skillet or wok.
2. Sauté the onion then add the vegetables, including the scallion or green onion, finely chopped hot pepper, salt, thyme and black pepper, add about 2 tablespoons water.
3. Cover and reduce the heat to low, stirring occasionally. Vegetables should be cooked within 10 minutes.

Serve on a bed of cooked rice.
Makes 4-6 servings.

# SALADS

Jamaican Salad...108

Cabbage & Carrot Salad...109

Carrot & Raisin Salad...110

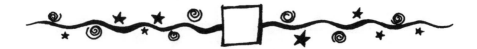

# JAMAICAN SALAD

1 lettuce
4 slices pineapple
½ cucumber
1 red sweet pepper
2 stalks scallion or
  spring onion

1. Wash the lettuce, drain and shred.
2. Dice the pineapple and cucumber.
3. Remove the seeds and slice the red pepper into thin strips.
4. Slice the spring onions.
5. Line a serving plate with the lettuce.
6. Combine the pineapple, red pepper, cucumber and spring onions and arrange on top of the lettuce.

Makes 4 servings.

# CABBAGE AND CARROT SALAD

½ cabbage, shredded
½ cucumber, sliced
2 medium-sized
   carrots, grated
½ cup beansprouts
3 medium sized
   tomatoes, thinly
   sliced
3 tablespoons salad oil
1 tablespoon vinegar
½ teaspoon freshly
   ground black pepper

1. Arrange the shredded cabbage on a serving dish.
2. Arrange the slices of cucumber around the edge of the dish.
3. Combine the grated carrots and beansprouts in a bowl and arrange in the centre of the dish.
4. Decorate with sliced tomatoes.
5. Mix the salad oil, vinegar and black pepper until well blended. Pour over salad and serve immediately.

# CARROT AND RAISIN SALAD

3 cups carrots, shredded

⅔ cup golden raisins

1 tablespoon orange juice

¼ cup mayonnaise

1 teaspoon ground nutmeg

¼ teaspoon salt

Black pepper to taste

1. Place the shredded carrots and raisins into a mixing bowl.
2. Add the orange juice and mix gently.
3. Gradually stir in the mayonnaise.
4. Add most of the ground nutmeg, salt and black pepper, mix well, ensuring that all the ingredients are evenly distributed.
5. Spoon into a serving bowl, sprinkle remaining nutmeg over salad and serve.

Makes 2-4 servings

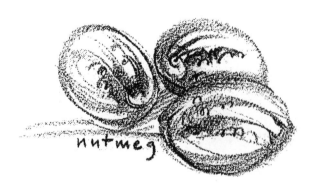

nutmeg

# VEGETABLES & LEGUMES

Rice & Peas...112

Candied Sweet Potatoes..113

Turned Cornmeal or Coo-Coo...114

Steamed Cabbage & Carrots...115

Irish Potato Casserole...116

Macaroni & Vegetables...117

Stewed Jackfruit...118

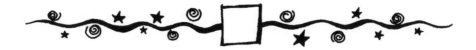

# RICE AND PEAS

*Rice and Peas is a major part of Jamaican cuisine. Because of its popularity in the Jamaican kitchen, it is called the "Jamaican Coat of Arms". In most households it is usually served on Sundays as part of the main course. Traditionally it is made with red peas, but can be made with gungo (pigeon) peas.*

1 cup dried red peas (kidney beans), soaked overnight

6 cups coconut milk or ⅓ block coconut cream mixed with 6 cups of water

2 cups rice, washed and drained

2 cloves garlic, crushed

2 stalks scallion, crushed

½ teaspoon salt

1 sprig or ¼ teaspoon thyme leaves

1 Scotch Bonnet pepper (unbroken)

1. Discard the water in which peas were soaked.
2. Boil the peas in the 6 cups of coconut milk until they are tender, but not over-cooked.
3. Add the garlic, scallion, salt, thyme, and unbroken Scotch Bonnet pepper.
4. Add the rice. The liquid should be at least 2 inches above the rice; add more water if necessary.
5. Stir with a fork and bring to the boil, then lower heat, cover and simmer for 20-30 minutes until the liquid is absorbed and the rice is tender.

Serve piping hot.

Make 4-6 servings.

NOTE: When cooking Rice and Peas use 2 cups of liquid to 1 cup of rice. For plain rice, use 1½ cups water to 1 cup of rice. Rice usually takes 25-30 minutes to cook. Do not stir rice while it's cooking or it will become soggy.

NOTE: Coconut cream is processed into a convenient block and sold in West Indian food stores.

# CANDIED SWEET POTATOES

*Sweet potatoes are quite versatile. They can be baked in the oven or on a charcoal fire, boiled, fried or used in a potato pudding.*

2 lbs sweet potatoes
4 tablespoons margarine
3 tablespoons dark sugar
¾ cup fresh orange juice
2 tablespoons Jamaican rum (optional)
¼ teaspoon grated nutmeg

1. Peel and wash the potatoes. Cut into slices about ½ inch thick.
2. Put in a saucepan and cover with cold water, bring to a boil over medium heat.
3. Boil for 20 minutes until tender, but not overcooked. Drain and set aside to cool.
4. Use 1 tablespoon of the margarine to grease a large, shallow ovenproof dish.
5. Melt the remaining margarine and pour over the potatoes and sprinkle with the sugar.
6. Pour orange juice and rum over the potatoes and sprinkle with nutmeg. Bake in the oven at 350° F for approximately 30 minutes. Serve immediately.

Makes 4 servings.

# TURNED CORNMEAL OR COO-COO

*This is the Jamaican version of the Barbadian Coo-Coo. The cornmeal is frequently used to make porridge or add to flour when making dumplings.*

1 oz salt pork (optional)
1 tablespoon cooking oil
1 onion, sliced thinly
1 large stalk scallion, minced
6 okras, sliced in rings
1 tomato, coarsely chopped
Few pieces of hot pepper cut very fine
5 cups coconut milk
½ cup salted codfish, shredded, and washed
2 cups cornmeal
Black pepper

1. Cut the salt pork into small pieces and fry them until golden brown. Set aside.
2. Sauté the onion and scallion in the same pan.
3. Add the okras, tomato and hot pepper and pour in the coconut milk.
4. Add the saltfish, thyme and salt pork.
5. Bring to a boil and simmer for about 10 minutes.
6. Gradually add the cornmeal, stirring to ensure there are no lumps.
7. Simmer for 15-20 minutes.

Serve with steamed fish.
Makes 4 servings.

# STEAMED CABBAGE AND CARROTS

*This makes an excellent side dish for any kind of meal.*

2 tablespoons margarine
1 large onion, finely chopped
1 cup water
1 small cabbage, shredded
2 carrots, shredded
1 teaspoon salt
½ teaspoon black pepper
Sprigs fresh thyme

1. Melt the butter and cook the onion until it is limp.
2. Add the water, cabbage, carrots, salt, pepper, and thyme. Bring to a brisk boil over a high heat.
3. Lower heat, cover and simmer, stirring occasionally until vegetables are tender and the water has evaporated.

Makes 2-4 servings.

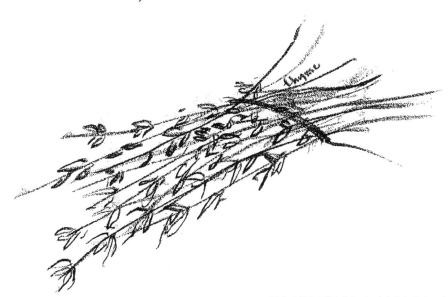

# IRISH POTATO CASSEROLE

*Jamaicans call white potatoes 'Irish' to differentiate them from their locally grown sweet potatoes. According to the records, Irish Potato comes from South America. It was not until 1719 that the potato was introduced to North America and Britain. Subsequently, it made its way to the Caribbean.*

6 medium potatoes
1½ tablespoon butter or
   margarine
1 large onion
Salt and pepper
1¼ cups milk

1. Peel, wash and slice potatoes thinly.
2. Slice the onion in thin rings.
3. Grease a shallow ovenproof dish with margarine or butter.
4. Arrange layers of potatoes and onion, sprinkling each layer with salt and black pepper. Dot with butter.
5. Pour milk over the potatoes and bake, uncovered, in a preheated oven at 375° F for 45 minutes or until they are tender.

Makes 2-4 servings.

# MACARONI AND VEGETABLES

1 cup elbow macaroni

3 tablespoons cooking oil

1 medium-sized onion, sliced thinly

1 small zucchini, sliced in rings

1 small cho-cho, cut into thin strips

2 medium carrots, cut into thin strips

Few pieces crushed Scotch bonnet pepper (seeds removed)

1 clove garlic, crushed

1 tablespoon butter

½ cup milk

1 tablespoon all purpose flour

1 cup grated cheddar cheese

1. Prepare macaroni according to the directions on the package. Drain.
2. Place in an oven proof dish and keep warm.
3. Heat the oil and sauté the onion, zucchini, cho cho, carrots, pieces of pepper and garlic until the vegetables are tender but still crisp.
4. Remove from heat and set aside.
5. Melt the butter in another saucepan over medium heat.
6. Combine the milk and flour and pour the mixture in the saucepan. Stir constantly until slightly thickened.
7. Remove saucepan from heat and stir in the cheese until it is melted. If the sauce is too thick add a little water or milk.
8. Combine sauce, vegetables and macaroni.

Serve immediately.
Makes 2-4 servings.

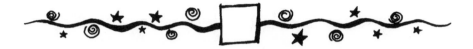

# STEWED JACKFRUIT

*When I was growing up in Jamaica, this dish was considered "poor people food" and not served to guests. I was pleasantly surprised when my friends from the Philippines and Pakistan told me that this is one of the most popular dishes in their countries!!*

*The jackfruit originates from the Indo-Malaysian region, but is found in most parts of the tropics. It is a member of the fig family and is related to the bread-fruit tree. Both have the same prickly skin but unlike breadfruits, jackfruits are attached close to the bark of the tree on short stalks. The jackfruit sometimes grow to a massive size and a single fruit can weigh up to forty pounds. It can be eaten when the fleshy inside is ripe or cooked when it is mature but not yet ripe,. When ripe, the fruits are very sweet and the smell is similar to ripe bananas, but a little stronger. The fleshy inside is full of seeds which can be roasted and eaten like chest-nuts or boiled with the fruit. Jackfruit seeds are delicious when cooked in 'peas' soup.*

1 large jackfruit
6 cups coconut milk
  (see recipe page 74)
1 onion, sliced thinly or
  2 stalks scallion,
  crushed
¼ teaspoon salt
1 tablespoon margarine
  or butter
2 sprigs fresh thyme
½ teaspoon black
  pepper
10 cups water

1. Cut jackfruit for easy handling. Remove the centre or heart, with a knife.
2. Remove the seeds and scrape them with a knife to remove the thin skin. Wash the flesh and seeds.
3. Place them in a saucepan with the water and cook until the seeds and flesh are tender and the water is absorbed.
4. Add the coconut milk, onion or scallion, thyme and salt. Continue cooking until the flesh becomes soft and only a small amount of liquid is left in the pot.

STEWED JACKFRUIT CONTINUED

5. Add the margarine or butter and sprinkle with black pepper. Mash with a wooden spoon. The seeds do not have to be crushed.
6. Simmer for another 5 minutes.

Serve hot or cold.

NOTE: When preparing this dish it's advisable not to wear your Sunday best because the jackfruit produces a sap which stains. To remove stains from your hands, use a household stain remover.

# ROOTS, FOOD AND TING

*In Jamaica, people often refer to root vegetables, green bananas and anything made with flour as 'Food'. It is not uncommon for someone, when served their main course with rice and salad, to ask for the "Food".*

Boiled Green Banana...121

Fried Dumplings or Johnny Cakes...121

Festival...122

Bammy...123

Breadfruit...124

Fried Ripe Plantains...125

# BOILED GREEN BANANAS

*This is good served with ackee and salted codfish or rundown.*

6 cups water
½ teaspoon salt
Vegetable oil
4-6 green bananas

1. Bring the water and salt to boil in a large pot. A little vegetable oil dropped in the water will prevent the bananas from becoming darkened by the high iron content in the skin.
2. Using a sharp knife cut off both ends of the bananas and score the skins deeply along their length.
3. Boil for 20 minutes until the bananas are soft.
4. Remove the skins.

# FRIED DUMPLINGS OR JOHNNY CAKES

*This is the only type of dumpling that is not cooked in soup or boiling water.*

1 cup flour
¼ teaspoon salt
1 teaspoon baking powder
Cold water
Cooking oil for frying

1. Mix flour, salt and baking powder together. Add cold water, a little at a time to form a dough and knead until smooth.
2. Divide the dough into equal portions. Shape into balls and flatten slightly.
3. Fry in moderately hot oil until the dumplings are golden brown.

Serve warm.

# FESTIVAL

*It is said that this pastry was created by a fisherman to celebrate Jamaica's annual Festival. This fried pastry is served with jerked meat or fried fish.*

1 cup all purpose flour
1 cup cornmeal
2 teaspoons sugar
¼ teaspoon salt
¼ teaspoon grated
   nutmeg
¼ teaspoon baking
   powder
½ teaspoon vanilla
½ cup milk
Oil for frying

1. Combine the first 7 ingredients in a large mixing bowl.
2. Add enough milk to hold the dry ingredients together, knead lightly to make a dough.
3. Divide dough into 6-8 portions, roll each portion into a sausage shape.
4. Heat a generous amount of oil in a deep skillet.
5. Fry festival until golden brown.

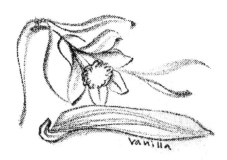

vanilla

# BAMMY

*Bammy is a bread made from the cassava tuber. There are two kinds of cassavas, the bitter and the sweet. Bitter cassava contains prussic acid and is primarily used for the production of starch and the 'bran' used to make a bammy. The sweet cassava is boiled and eaten as a vegetable or used to make pone or pudding. Bammies are produced commercially in Jamaica and exported to other countries including Canada where they are available in Jamaican food stores.*

Bammies

1. Soak the bammies in coconut milk or cow's milk until they absorb the liquid.
2. Cut each bammy in 4 pieces and brush with margarine.
3. Place the bammies on a baking sheet and place in the oven preheated to 350° F.
4. Bake for 15-20 minutes or until the bammies are tender.

Serve warm.

# BREADFRUIT

*Traditionally, breadfruit is roasted on charcoal or firewood. Here are two easy ways you can cook it in your kitchen.*

1 breadfruit, mature but not ripe (Jamaicans say it's 'fit')

**Roasted**

1. Remove the stem.
2. Rub the outside with a little oil and bake in the oven for 30-45 minutes at 350° F. If an inserted knife goes in without any resistance the fruit is cooked.
3. Remove from the oven and cool.
4. Peel and cut in half. Remove the centre or heart and discard. Cut the breadfruit in slices.

Serve with run down.

**Boiled**

1. Cut the breadfruit into slices, peel, remove the heart and discard.
2. Boil the breadfruit in salted water much like potatoes or cook it in soups.

# FRIED RIPE PLANTAINS

3-4 plantains
Cooking oil for frying

1. Cut the plantain in half, then cut each half lengthwise into 4 strips.
2. Fry them in hot oil until golden brown.
3. Drain well on paper towels.

Serve warm.
Makes 4-6 servings

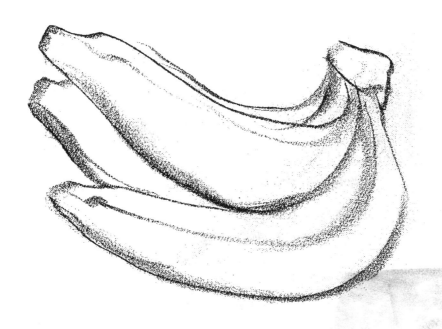

# PASTRIES, PORRIDGES & DESSERTS

# JAMAICAN PASTRIES

Personally, I do not have a sweet tooth, which is most likely a reflection of the household in which I grew up. Pastries were not too popular in our home. Occasionally my mother would make sweet potato pudding, gizadas, coconut biscuits or dukunoo. Dukunoo, also known as "tie-a-leaf" or "blue drawers", is a dough made from cornmeal, sugar and spices which is wrapped in banana leaves, tied with a string and boiled. Mostly, we ate a lot of fresh fruits such as mangoes, bananas, guavas, rose apples, otaheite apples — to name a few. The parish of St Ann, where I was born, is named the 'garden parish'. There are hardly any fruits in Jamaica that are not grown in St. Ann.

Below are a few of the pastry recipes that were given to me by my mother.

Jamaican Sweet Potato Pudding or Pone...129

Cornmeal Pone or Pudding...130

Tie-a-leaf (Blue Drawers)...131

Corn Cake...132

Cassava Pone or Pudding...133

Coconut Toto...134

Bulla Cake...135

Gizadas...136

Coconut Biscuits (Jackass Corn)...137

Jean's Easter Buns Without Yeast...138

Marcia's Corn Bread...139

# JAMAICAN SWEET POTATO PUDDING OR PONE

*Do not use a food processor or the shredder side of a grater to grate potatoes and coco. The food processor will make the mixture too watery and the shredder side will make them coarse in texture.*

2 lbs sweet potatoes, peeled and washed

1 coco, peeled and washed

¼ cup flour

¼ cup cornmeal

1½ cups brown sugar

1 teaspoon powdered cinnamon

¼ teaspoon grated nutmeg

¼ teaspoon salt

¼ lb raisins (optional)

2 teaspoons vanilla

1 tablespoon butter

3 cups coconut milk

1. Grate the sweet potatoes and coco.
2. Combine the grated potatoes, coco, flour, cornmeal, sugar, spices, salt, raisins, vanilla and butter. Mix in the coconut milk.
3. Pour the mixture into a greased baking pan or oven proof dish and cover.
4. Bake in the oven at 350° F for 1 hour and 20 minutes.
5. Insert a knife in the middle of the pudding, if the knife comes out clean, the pudding is done.

Cool before serving.
Makes 12 servings.

# CORNMEAL PONE OR PUDDING

6 cups coconut milk or
cow's milk

1 cup brown sugar

3 cups cornmeal

½ cup flour

1 tablespoon vanilla

½ teaspoon grated
nutmeg

½ cup raisins

¼ cup rum (optional)

¼ teaspoon salt

1 tablespoon butter

1. Mix the sugar and milk together and stir until the sugar is almost dissolved.
2. Mix together the cornmeal and flour in a large bowl. Stir in the milk mixture.
3. Add vanilla, nutmeg, raisins, rum and salt. Mix.
4. Pour into a greased baking dish.
5. Dot butter on top of the mixture, cover and bake at 375° F for approximately 1½ hours or until an inserted knife comes out clean.

Makes 12 servings

# TIE-A-LEAF (BLUE DRAWERS)

*My sister-in-law, who is from Africa and now lives in Jamaica, said this pastry originated in West Africa and is called Kenke.*

*I was asked, on several occasions, to include this recipe in the book, but my response was "we don't have any banana leaves up here in Canada". I was told that the banana leaf is available in Chinese food stores. However, if the banana leaf is not available, cooking bags are a good substitute.*

½ cup flour
2 cups cornmeal
½ cup brown sugar
½ teaspoon salt
½ teaspoon vanilla
1 teaspoon powdered cinnamon
1 teaspoon grated nutmeg
2½ cups coconut milk or cow's milk

1. Mix together the flour and cornmeal in a large bowl.
2. In another bowl mix together the sugar, salt, vanilla, cinnamon, nutmeg and milk. Stir until the sugar is dissolved.
3. Combine the milk mixture with the dry ingredients.
4. Pour ½ cup of the mixture into cooking bags or onto pieces of banana leaf 8"x 6". Make parcels and tie with a string.
5. Place in a large pot of boiling water to cover and simmer for 40 minutes.

Remove from packets and serve. Tie-a-leaf is best eaten when warm and fresh but can be eaten cold.
Makes 6 servings

# CORN CAKE

3 cups skim milk
4 tablespoons brown
  sugar
½ teaspoon vanilla
1 cup cornmeal
2 eggs
Pinch of salt
2 tablespoons
  margarine

1. Grease and line the bottom of a 7 inch pan with a circle of waxed paper.
2. Place the milk, sugar and vanilla into a saucepan and bring to a boil.
3. Stir in the cornmeal quickly to avoid lumps.
4. Remove the pan from the heat and allow to cool slightly.
5. Separate the eggs. Beat the egg whites with a pinch of salt until they form a peak. Set aside.
6. Add the margarine and egg yolks, one at a time, to the cornmeal and beat well.
7. Stir in one spoonful of the egg white and then fold in the remainder carefully.
8. Pour the mixture into the prepared pan and bake at 350° F for about 40 minutes.
9. Transfer the cake onto a cake rack and cool. Decorate with fresh fruits.

Makes 6-8 servings

# CASSAVA PONE OR PUDDING

2 lbs sweet cassava,
peeled and grated
1 coconut, grated to
make 3 cups milk
(see recipe page 74)
1 teaspoon vanilla
½ teaspoon grated
nutmeg
1 cup sugar

1. In large bowl combine the grated cassava and coconut milk.
2. Gradually mix in the vanilla, nutmeg and sugar until you have a soft but thick batter, add a little water or cow's milk if necessary.
3. Pour the mixture into a greased baking dish and bake in a moderately hot oven at 350º F for 1 hour.

Makes 6-8 servings

vanilla

# COCONUT TOTO

¼ lb butter, unsalted

½ cup granulated sugar

½ cup light brown sugar

2 cups flour

2 teaspoons baking powder

1 teaspoon ground cinnamon

2 cups grated coconut

¼ teaspoon grated nutmeg

2 teaspoons vanilla

½ cup coconut milk

1 egg, beaten

1. Cream the butter with the sugars.
2. Combine the flour, baking powder, cinnamon, grated coconut and nutmeg. Add to the butter and sugar mixture.
3. Add the vanilla, milk and beaten egg. Mix to a stiff paste.
4. Spread evenly in a greased, shallow baking tin and bake at 350° F for 30 to 35 minutes until golden.
5. Cool and cut into squares.

Makes 9 squares

# BULLA CAKE

*These were the most popular local cakes when I was growing up in Jamaica. They used to be made by bakers and sold to the shops in the district. It was a treat to eat bulla cake, especially with avocado pear. I would bite a piece of bulla and bite a piece of pear and chew them both together. It was delicious! Bulla cake is sold in Jamaican food stores in Canada.*

3 cups flour
2 teaspoons baking powder
½ teaspoon salt
1 teaspoon grated nutmeg
1 teaspoon grated fresh ginger
3 tablespoons melted butter
1 cup dark sugar dissolved in 1 cup water

1. Combine the flour, baking powder, salt and nutmeg.
2. Mix in the grated ginger, melted butter and enough of the sugar and water solution to make a firm dough.
3. Knead the dough on a lightly floured board.
4. Roll out ½" thick and cut into rounds, using a saucer or cookie cutter.
5. Lift off with spatula and place on a greased, floured baking tray.
6. Bake in a preheated oven at 375° F for 20-25 minutes.

Makes 6-8 bullas.

# GIZADAS

*This is one of my mother's favourites. When I visit her in Jamaica, she makes sure I bring back her homemade Gizadas and Coconut Biscuits.*

**The coconut syrup mixture**

½ cup brown sugar
½ cup water
1 coconut, grated
1 teaspoon rose water
½ teaspoon grated nutmeg
1 teaspoon ground cinnamon

**The Pastry**

1 cup flour
¼ teaspoon salt
½ cup shortening
cold water

1. Make a syrup by combining the brown sugar and water in a saucepan and cooking over a low heat.
2. Add the grated coconut to the boiled syrup, then mix in the rose water, nutmeg and cinnamon.
3. Remove from heat and set aside.
4. Stir together the flour and salt, add the shortening and combine it with the flour.
5. Pour in some water, mixing in a little at a time until the pastry looks like a dough.
6. Roll the dough slightly thicker than you would normally for tarts.
7. Use a teacup to make circles in the dough and cut out rounds with a knife.
8. Pinch the edges to form a ridge or flute at the edges of the pastry. Cases should be about ½" high.
9. Fill each case with the coconut mixture.
10. Bake on a cookie sheet at 375° F for 35 minutes.

Makes 6-8 servings

# COCONUT BISCUITS (JACKASS CORN)

*These cookies become crisp when cool.*

½ cup brown sugar
1 coconut, grated
¼ teaspoon salt
¼ teaspoon grated
  nutmeg
1 teaspoon baking
  powder
1 cup flour

1. Combine brown sugar and grated coconut.
2. Add salt, nutmeg, baking powder and flour.
3. Knead the ingredients together until a dough is formed.
4. Sprinkle a little flour on a pastry board and roll the dough fairly thin.
5. Cut into 2″ rounds.
6. Bake on a greased tray at 375° F for 10-12 minutes.

Makes 6 servings.

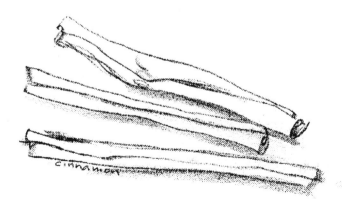

# JEAN'S EASTER BUNS WITHOUT YEAST

*This recipe is from Jean, one of my life-time girlfriends.*
*It is a version of the English "hot cross buns" but a little more spicy. It is tradition-ally eaten with cheese on Good Friday.*

2 tablespoon margarine
  or butter
1 cup dark sugar
½ cup honey
1 bottle stout
2 eggs, beaten
3 cups all purpose flour
3 teaspoons baking
  powder
½ teaspoon salt
1 teaspoon vanilla
1 teaspoon allspice
½ teaspoon grated
  nutmeg
1 cup raisins, currants
  and mixed peel
  combined
1 teaspoon vanilla

1. Dissolve the margarine, sugar, honey and stout over a low heat.
2. Remove from heat and allow to cool.
3. Beat the eggs and add to the liquid mixture.
4. In a bowl, combine flour, baking powder, salt, vanilla and spices.
5. Stir the stout mixture into the dry ingredients.
6. Add the raisins, currants and mixed peel. Combine to make a stiff dough.
7. Shape into loaves and put into greased loaf tins.
8. Bake in a preheated oven at 350° F or until an inserted knife comes out clean.

Makes 12 slices

# MARCIA'S CORN BREAD

*This recipe is from my daughter, Marcia. She usually serves this as a side dish with barbequed chicken or jerked pork.*

1 cup flour
2 teaspoons baking powder
¼ teaspoon salt
1 cup cornmeal
4 tablespoons sugar
2 eggs, beaten
1 cup milk
¼ cup butter

1. Combine flour, baking powder and salt.
2. Add the cornmeal and sugar to the dry ingredients.
3. Stir in the beaten eggs, milk and butter, mixing well until the batter is smooth.
4. Pour into a greased loaf tin and bake in preheated oven at 350° F for 25-30 minutes or until an inserted knife comes out clean.

Makes 6 servings

# PORRIDGES

As an adult I now realize how well we were fed during our childhood. My mother told me that, as babies, after we were weaned from breast milk we were fed porridge prepared with fresh cow's or goat's milk. No spices or salt were added to the baby's porridge. As we grew up we continued to eat porridge, but spiced with cinnamon or nutmeg.

Cornmeal Porridge...141

Banana Porridge...142

Hominy...143

# CORNMEAL PORRIDGE

1 cup cornmeal

3 cups cold water

¼ teaspoon salt

1 cup cow or goat's milk

1 teaspoon vanilla

2 cinnamon leaves or a small piece of cinnamon stick

¼ teaspoon grated nutmeg

½ cup sugar

1. Mix the cornmeal with a little of the cold water to make a paste.
2. In a saucepan, bring the remainder of the water to a boil, add the salt and stir in the cornmeal.
3. Bring to a boil, stirring constantly.
4. Lower the heat and continue cooking for about 10 minutes.
5. Stir in the milk, vanilla, cinnamon, nutmeg and sugar.
6. Add extra milk if too thick.
7. Simmer for another 5 minutes.

Serve in bowls and sprinkle with grated nutmeg on top.

Makes 6 servings

NOTE: 1 cup coconut milk can be used instead of cow or goat's milk

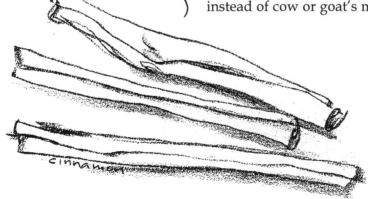

cinnamon

# BANANA PORRIDGE

3 green bananas, grated
4 cups water
2 tablespoons flour
1 cup milk
½ teaspoon nutmeg
1 teaspoon vanilla
¼ teaspoon salt (optional)
½ cup sugar

1. Add the water and flour to the grated bananas and beat the mixture well until it is lump-free.
2. Pour into a saucepan and bring to a boil, then lower heat and simmer for 15 minutes, stirring occasionally.
3. Pour in the milk and add the nutmeg, vanilla, salt and sugar.
4. Continue to simmer for another 5 minutes, stirring well.

Serve in bowls and sprinkle with grated nutmeg.

Makes 6 servings

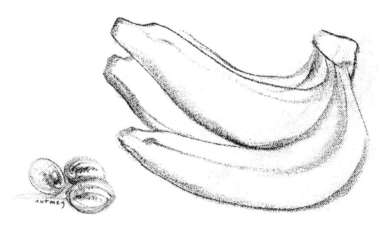

# HOMINY

*The hominy corn is sold, already prepared, in Jamaican and West Indian food stores. Previously, my mother would soak the corn in a natural lye of ashes mixed with water. The lye made it easy to remove the film-like skin from the dried corn.*

1 cup hominy corn
Water
2 cups coconut milk or
   cow's milk
2 tablespoons cornflour
¼ teaspoon salt
   (optional)
½ teaspoon grated
   nutmeg
1 teaspoon vanilla
1 cup sugar

1. Wash the corn, place in a pot with water to cover and boil for 1½ hours until the corn is soft.
2. Mix the coconut milk or cow's milk with the cornflour. Pour the mixture into the pot and add salt.
3. Simmer for 15 minutes, stirring continuously as the mixture thickens.
4. Add the spices, vanilla and sugar. Stir and simmer for another 5 minutes.

Serve in a bowl with grated nutmeg sprinkled on top.
Makes 4 servings.

# FRUITS FOR DESSERTS

It is said that when Christopher Columbus came to Jamaica at the end of the fifteenth century, he thought he had found the Garden of Eden. His diaries record the richness of the vegetation and the great variety of strange and colourful fruits he found there. In recent years there has been a migration of people, fruits and vegetables from Jamaica to other parts of the world. Fruits such as naseberries, mangoes, guavas, avocados, papaya, pineapple, plantain, to name a few, are becoming more familiar to the inhabitants of North America and Europe.

Baked Ripe Banana...145

Fruit Flan...146

Tropical Fruit Salad...147

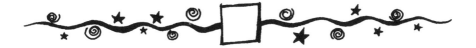

# BAKED RIPE BANANA

*Serve these warm with vanilla ice cream for a simple but delicious dessert.*

4 large ripe bananas
¼ cup margarine
1-2 tablespoons honey
4 tablespoons lime or
    orange juice
½ teaspoon allspice

1. Peel the bananas and slice each into two, lengthwise.
2. Grease a shallow oven proof dish with a little of the margarine.
3. Arrange the bananas in the dish.
4. Mix together the honey and lime or orange juice.
5. Pour the mixture over the banana slices and sprinkle with the allspice.
6. Dot with the remaining margarine.
7. Bake at 200° F for 15-20 minutes.

Makes 2-4 servings

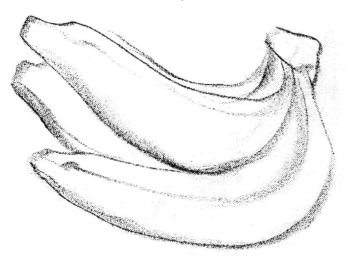

# FRUIT FLAN

*This dessert makes a perfect finale for any festive meal.*

**Flan shell**

½ package shortbread mix, or prepared pie shell

¼ cup soft butter

**Filling**

18 oz package cream cheese, softened

½ cup icing sugar

1 teaspoon vanilla

½ cup whipping cream

4 cups fresh or canned fruits

1. Combine shortbread mix with butter according to the directions on the package.
2. Press dough into an 11" pan and prick well with a fork.
3. Chill in the refrigerator for 15 minutes.
4. Bake at 425° F for 5-8 minutes or until light golden. Set aside to cool.
5. Beat cream cheese, icing sugar and vanilla together until smooth.
6. In a separate bowl, whip cream until stiff. Fold into the cheese mixture.
7. Spread evenly in the prepared shell, chill for 15 minutes.
8. Arrange fruits attractively on the top.

Makes 4 servings.

# TROPICAL FRUIT SALAD

*This is as eye-appealing as it is delicious — made with your choice of fresh Island fruits.*

1 lb watermelon, sliced, seeded and cut in wedges

1 small pineapple, peeled and cut in 2" slices, reserve the top for decoration

1 papaya, peeled and sliced

2 mangoes, peeled and sliced

2 tangerines, peeled and sliced

2 bananas, sliced, skins removed

½ cup passion fruit syrup

1. Place the pineapple top in the centre of a serving dish.
2. Arrange the fruits attractively in circles around the pineapple.
3. Pour over the passion fruit syrup and serve immediately.

Makes 4-8 servings.

# DRINKS
# &
# BEVERAGES

# NON-ALCOHOLIC BEVERAGES OR JAMAICAN 'SKY JUICE'

You might not want to buy store bought drinks after trying these home-made ones.

Jamaican Ginger Apple Drink...151

Mango Drink...151

Soursop & Lime Shake...152

Ginger Drink...152

Carrot Drink...153

Sorrel or Jamaican Flowers Drink...154

Limeade or Lemonade...155

Irish Moss Drink...156

Egg Nog...157

# JAMAICAN GINGER APPLE DRINK

6 apples
1 cup granulated sugar
1 cup grated ginger
10 cups water

1. Wash apples and cut in small pieces.
2. Bring the water to boil in a large pot.
3. Add the apples and ginger and boil for 15 minutes or until the apples are tender.
4. Remove from heat and cool. Strain through a sieve or cheesecloth.
5. Sweeten to taste.

Serve over crushed ice.
Makes 6-10 servings

# MANGO DRINK

6 mangoes
10 cups boiling water
¼ cup lime juice
½ cup granulated sugar

1. Peel the mangoes and cut away the flesh from the stone.
2. Pour boiling water over the mangoes and allow to stand until the water is cold.
3. Press through a sieve to make a puree.
4. Add lime juice and sweeten to taste.

Chill and serve over crushed ice.
Makes 6-10 servings

# SOURSOP AND LIME SHAKE

*If you use the condensed milk leave out the lime.*

1 medium soursop
4 cups hot water
¼ teaspoon grated
  nutmeg
1 teaspoon vanilla
Juice of 2 medium
  limes
1 cup sugar or ½ cup
  condensed milk

1. Remove the skin and seeds of the soursop.
2. Place the flesh in a bowl.
3. Pour over the hot water and allow to cool.
4. Press the soaked fruit through a sieve. Retain the liquid and discard the thrash.
5. Stir in nutmeg, vanilla and lime juice and sweeten with sugar or condensed milk.

Makes 2-4 servings.

# GINGER DRINK

*Jamaica is sometimes called the "Land of Ginger". It is famous for the production and exportation of the finest ginger in the world.*
*This simple way of making a quick and delicious ginger drink was brought from Jamaica by my niece, Laura.*

1 lb fresh Jamaican
  ginger, cleaned,
  grated or crushed
10 cups boiling water
2 cups brown sugar
Juice of 1 lime

1. Place the ginger in a pot or large heat proof dish. Pour the boiling water over ginger.
2. Cover and steep overnight.
3. Next day strain, add lime juice and sweeten to taste.

Serve over crushed ice.
Makes 6-10 servings.

# CARROT DRINK

*This is a wonderfully refreshing drink, nourishing too, as carrots are a high source of carotene.*

8 medium sized carrots, grated or chopped in a blender

3 cups water

Juice of 1 lime (do not use lime juice if you use condensed milk)

3 tablespoons sugar or ¼ cup condensed milk

¼ teaspoon grated nutmeg

1 tablespoon rum or sherry (optional)

1. If a blender is used, cut the carrots in small pieces.
2. Place in the blender, adding small amounts at a time, using up the 3 cups of cold water, adjust to grate for 30 seconds.
3. Squeeze by hand and strain as you would for coconut.
4. Discard the thrash or use to make carrot cake.
5. Add the lime juice, sugar and nutmeg, mix.
6. Add rum or sherry (optional) .

Makes 2 servings.

nutmeg

# SORREL OR JAMAICAN FLOWERS DRINK

*Sorrel, known as Hibiscus Flowers by Jamaicans and Roselle in the Eastern Caribbean is combined with ginger to make a delicious drink. Very popular in Jamaica especially at Christmas time, it is usually accompanied with Christmas cake during one's rounds of holiday visits.*

8 cups dried sorrel
　petals
½ cup grated ginger
2 dozen pimento seeds
12 cups boiling water
¼ cup rum to preserve
Sugar to taste

1. Place the sorrel petals, ginger and pimento seeds in a large pot. Pour the boiling water over.
2. Cover and leave to steep overnight.
3. Next day strain through a sieve or cheesecloth.
4. Add rum and sugar to sweeten.
5. Pour into bottles and refrigerate.

Makes 10-12 servings.

# LIMEADE (COMMONLY KNOWN AS LEMONADE)

*This thirst-quenching drink is a popular non-alcoholic drink in Jamaica.*
*Lime trees are grown in most backyards in Jamaica and are more abundant than*
*lemons. Lemonade is usually made with limes so I think it is more realistic to name*
*the drink "Limeade".*

6 cups water
½ cup freshly squeezed
   lime juice
1 ½ cups brown sugar

1. Pour water into a jug and add the lime juice and sugar.
2. Mix well until the sugar is dissolved.
3. Serve very cold or with crushed ice.

NOTE: Add some beer to the limeade and you will get another Jamaican drink called "Shandy Dandy".
Makes 4-6 servings.

# IRISH MOSS DRINK

*This jelly-like substance is made from a seaweed, generally known in Jamaica as 'Irish Moss'. It is said that this drink has aphrodisiac qualities. The Irish moss drink is commercially produced in Jamaica, and sold in bottles or cans and is available in Jamaican food stores.*

2 oz dried Irish Moss
10 cups water
Condensed milk to
   sweeten
¼ teaspoon grated
   nutmeg
1 tablespoon Jamaican
   rum (optional)

1. Wash and soak Irish moss until it becomes limp. Discard water.
2. Pour 10 cups cold water into a deep saucepan. Add the moss.
3. Simmer until the moss is tender and the liquid resembles a thin syrup. Add more water to achieve desired quantity or thickness.
4. Strain the liquid through a fine sieve.
5. Add condensed milk to sweeten, nutmeg and rum.

Chill before serving.
Makes 6-10 servings.

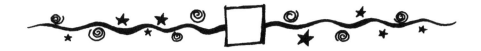

# EGG NOG

*This drink is traditionally served during the Christmas season.*

6 eggs
2 cups sugar
3 cups milk
½ cup rum
1 teaspoon grated
   nutmeg
Vanilla

1. Beat the eggs.
2. Gradually add the sugar, milk, rum, nutmeg and vanilla.

Serve on crushed ice.
Makes 4 servings.

vanilla

# ALCOHOLIC BEVERAGES

Rum is synonymous with Jamaica. Made from molasses, a by-product of sugar, Jamaican rum ranges from light amber to dark gold, each with its own taste and qualities. The rum drunk in Jamaica is stronger and subtler in flavour than those generally available in Canada and other European countries, which are imported in bulk and then blended. All rum, whether distilled from cane juice or molasses, comes from sugar-cane. As kids our version of a candy bar was chewing and sucking the sweet juice from a cane stalk.

Jamaican Rum Punch...159

Jamaican Planter's Punch...159

Banana Daiquiri...160

Pina Colada...160

Brown Cow...161

Jamaican Coffee...161

# JAMAICAN RUM PUNCH

*The basic procedure for making Jamaica's famous rum punch is as follows:*

1 part sour = 1 cup
   lime juice
2 parts sweet = 2 cups
   strawberry syrup
3 parts strong = 3 cups
   white rum
4 parts weak = 4 cups
   water or fruit juice
1 dozen pimento seeds

1. Mix the first 4 ingredients together.
2. Add the pimento seeds.

~~~~~~~~~~~~~~~~~~~~~~~

Serve on crushed ice.
NOTE: The strength increases when stored
   in bottles and left to ferment for days or
   weeks.
Makes 10-12 servings.

# JAMAICAN PLANTER'S PUNCH

4 tablespoons
   granulated sugar
1 tablespoon lime juice
4 tablespoons water
8 tablespoons rum
2 slices pineapple
Crushed ice
2 cherries

1. Combine the sugar, lime juice, water and
   rum, mix well until the sugar is dissolved.
2. Chop the pineapple into small pieces
   and add to the liquid. Mix well.

~~~~~~~~~~~~~~~~~~~~~~~

Serve on crushed ice and decorate with the
   cherries.
Makes 2-4 servings.

# BANANA DAIQUIRI

½ cup white rum
2 tablespoons fine
    white sugar
⅓ cup fresh lime juice
1 banana, sliced
2½ cups crushed ice
Chill 2 cocktail glasses

1. Place the rum, sugar, lime juice, sliced banana and crushed ice into a food processor and blend for 30 seconds.
2. Pour into cocktail glasses and serve immediately.

# PINA COLADA

4 oz dark rum
1 5oz can of pineapple
    juice
2 oz bottled coconut
    syrup
2 oz fresh lime juice
3 or 4 ice cubes

1. Blend all the ingredients in a blender until smooth.
2. Pour into tall glasses with ice and serve at once.

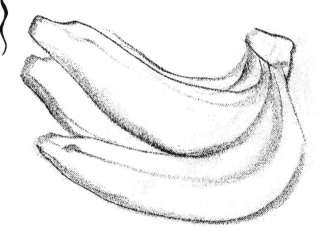

# COFFEE DRINKS

*Jamaica grows the famous "Blue Mountain" coffee in the hills of Surrey County in the eastern part of the island. It is considered by many coffee connoisseurs to be one of the world's finest. Jamaicans are proud of it but find it something of a luxury since so much of the crop is exported to Japan. Jamaica's famous liqueur, Tia Maria, is flavoured with Blue Mountain coffee and is perhaps the Island's single best known export.*

## BROWN COW

2 oz Tia Maria
2 oz milk

1. Mix Tia Maria and milk together.

Serve with crushed ice.
Makes 1 serving.

## JAMAICAN COFFEE

4 cups hot, strong Blue
   Mountain coffee
2 tablespoons sugar
½ cup rum
½ whipped cream

1. Combine the first 3 ingredients and mix well.
2. Pour into 4 mugs and spoon the whipped cream on top.

Makes 4 servings.

# GLOSSARY

## A

**Ackee:** The fruit of a West African tree brought to Jamaica by African slaves. When ripe the pear—shaped pods split open, exposing the edible yellow-fleshed fruit, each with a glossy black seed. The unripe ackee contains a poisonous substance called hypoglycine. Canned ackees are exported and can be purchased at Jamaican and Caribbean foodstores.

**Allspice (Pimento):** Berry of the pimento tree. The tree is indigenous to Jamaica. The flavour of the berries is similar to a combination of nutmeg, cinnamon and cloves. Allspice is one of the prime ingredients in jerked pork.

**Annato:** The seeds are orangy-red in colour and are traditionally used to colour stews, soups and fish dishes. The seeds are often seeped in oil which takes the colour of the annato.

**Avocado or 'Pear':** A tropical pear-shaped fleshy fruit. It's served as an accompaniment to main courses and in salads. The avocado is also widely used in skin products.

## B

**Bake:** To cook by dry heat, usually in an oven.

**Barbecue:** Generally refers to foods cooked outdoors over an open fire with spicy sauce.

**Baste:** To brush or spoon liquid over food while cooking, to keep it moist.

**Batter**: Any combination which includes flour, milk, butter, eggs or the like for pancakes, coating, dipping, etc.

**Beat**: To mix with a whisk beater or spoon so as to make the mixture smooth.

**Blend**: To mix two or more ingredients thoroughly.

**Breadfruit**: A large round green fruit with a greenish bumpy skin. When mature the flesh is creamy. The breadfruit can be roasted, baked, boiled or fried. The most refined variety is the `yellow heart'.

**Broccoli**: A vegetable of the mustard family, related to the cabbage and cauliflower.

## C

**Callaloo**: A vegetable similar to spinach. It is one of the main ingredients in the Jamaican Pepperpot soup and can be eaten steamed, sauteed or cooked with salted cod.

**Cassava**: A tropical plant with a fleshy white root. There are two kinds, the bitter and the sweet. The bitter cassava is primarily used for the production of starch. After the starch is removed the 'bran' is used for making a bread called "bammy". The sweet cassava is boiled like yam. Sweet cassava is also used for making pone.

**Casserole**: Covered glass or earthen dish in which food is baked and served.

**Cayenne**: Dried, powdered hot pepper.

**Chestnut**: A tree of the beech family, bearing nuts in a prickly bur.

**Cho cho**: Also known as Chayote, English Squash and Christophene, it grows on a vine and resembles a large pear, and is related to the squash family. It can be green or white with deep ribbings. In Jamaica, the cho cho is either boiled and served as an accompaniment to meat dishes or included in soups and stews. It is said that the juice has been used to reduce hypertension

**Cinnamon**: The sticks of the cinnamon plant is used to flavour puddings and porridges. They are also used to flavour drinks and liqueurs.

**Coat**: To cover the entire surface of food with flour or bread crumbs.

**Co co**: Also known as tania. It is a starchy tuber and is usually boiled or added to soups. Co co is similar to dasheen, a member of the same family of tubers.

**Coconut**: A member of the palm family of plants. The water inside the coconut is a favourite cooling drink in Jamaica. It is often confused with the milk which is made by adding water to grated coconut and pressing it through a sieve. Coconut milk provides an important flavouring in dishes such as rice and peas. A hammer or heavy object is used to break the hard shell of the coconut.

**Corn**: Maize or Indian corn. It is eaten on the cob, grilled or boiled. Cornmeal (ground, dried corn) can be added to flour when making dumplings, or made into corn bread, pudding, cake, or a thick, sweetened, spiced porridge. The dried corn is also used to make Hominy.

**Cream**: To combine butter or other shortening with sugar using a wooden spoon or mixer until light and fluffy.

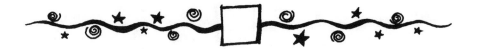

## D

**Deep fry**: To cook in deep hot fat or oil which covers the food until crispy and golden.

**Dice**: To cut into small cubes.

**Deseed**: Remove seeds.

**Devein**: Remove veins.

**Dot**: To scatter small bits of butter of margarine over the surface of food.

**Dumplings**: Jamaican dumplings do not contain yeast. They are flat and round in shape. They can be fried or boiled and may be served as an accompaniment to ackee and salt fish, run down, and in soups. When frying dumplings, a little baking powder is added to the flour.

## E

**Egg Plant:** Jamaicans call it "Garden Egg" and it is also known as Aubergine. It is not a popular vegetable in Jamaica. The vegetables are large with a purple colour and pear—shaped.

**Escallion**: Belongs to the same family as onion, garlic and chives. It is similar to green onion in appearance, but its flavour is stronger. It is popularly used in Jamaican cooking, especially in soups.

## F

**Fricasseed Chicken**: Chicken pieces seasoned with onion, garlic, escallion, salt and black pepper. It is marinaded overnight. Next day the chicken is browned in hot oil and stewed in gravy.

**Fritters**: Fried cakes made of batter, often containing pieces of salted cod.

**Fry**: To cook in hot fat using moderate to high heat.

## G

**Glaze**: A thin coating of beaten egg, milk and syrup which is brushed over pastry, fruits, ham, chicken, etc.

**Grate**: To rub food against a grater to form small particles.

**Gungo Peas**: Also known as pigeon or congo peas. Used in soups, stews or cooked in rice.

## I

**Irish Moss**: A seaweed or algae. It is boiled and made into a drink.

**Irish Potato**: White potato. Originally from South America and known as "Irish" in Jamaica to differentiate it from the sweet potato.

## K

**Knead**: To work dough with your hands until it is of the desired elasticity or consistency.

## L

**Lime**: Similar to lemon but the flavour is stronger.

## M

**Marinade**: Liquid used for seasoning by soaking, usually a mixture of oil, wine and seasonings.

**Marinate**: To soak in a marinade to tenderize or add flavour.

**Mango**: One of Jamaicans' favourite fruits. The tree is evergreen and is grown as a fruit and shade tree. When ripe the colours range from green to yellow—red with a yellow juicy flesh encasing a large seed. There are many varieties.

## O

**Offal**: Parts of pigs, goats, cattle, and poultry which are cut away from the meat and bone.

**Oxtail**: The tail of the cow.

## P

**Papaya**: The Jamaican pronunciation is "Paw Paw". When ripe it is yellow or orange with a soft orange flesh and shiny grey or black seeds. It is eaten raw with a squeeze of lime juice or included in fruit salad. Most parts of the tree contain papain, a digestive enzyme used as a meat tenderizer.

**Paprika**: Red sweet pepper dried and ground.

**Parboil**: To boil until partly cooked.

**Passion Fruit**: Most often green—yellow in colour and hard—shelled. When opened, the fruit shows a mass of seeds surrounded by fleshy pulp. It makes an excellent drink or syrup.

**Patties**: Tasty meat and pastry snacks.

**Peppers**: The most popular hot pepper in Jamaica is the "Scotch bonnet," which has a distinctive and delicious flavour. Care should be taken when handling them; do not touch your face

or eyes after working with them. Be sure to wash your hands thoroughly afterwards.

**Pickapeppa**: Jamaican hot pepper sauce which is processed in natural cane—vinegar then fermented and blended to give the sauce a tangy flavour.

**Pineapple**: The plant has spiny leaves, bearing a large, edible, juicy fruit. It was introduced to Jamaica by the Spanish from Central and South America and is called "Pine" in Jamaica.

**Preheat**: To turn oven on at a selected temperature to warm 10 minutes before it is needed.

**Puree**: To press through a sieve or put through a food blender to produce a smooth texture.

# R

**Reduce**: To cook over a high heat, uncovered, until the liquid is reduced and the food is a desired consistency.

**Red Peas or Kidney Beans**: These are the most popular peas in Jamaica. They are used in soups, stews and rice dishes.

**Red Stripe Beer**: Jamaican domestic beer.

**Roast:** To cook meat by dry heat, in an oven or on a spit.

# S

**Salted Cod**: Used in many of the traditional Jamaican dishes. Available on the bone or filletted and wrapped in plastic packages. Available in Jamaican foodstores and some Italian foodstores.

**Saute**: To fry lightly in a small amount of fat, turning and stirring frequently.

**Scald**: To pour boiling water over foods.

**Score**: To cut narrow gashes on the surface of foods.

**Shred**: To cut into fine strips.

**Simmer**: To cook liquid just below boiling point.

**Soursop**: A heart-shaped fruit with a skin. The flesh is white and makes a delicious drink and ice cream.

**Stew**: A long, slow method of cooking in liquid in a covered pan, to tenderize tough meats.

**Stir**: To blend ingredients with a circular motion.

**Sweet Potato**: A perennial tuberous root. In the U.S.A. it is referred to as yam, but is not related. Sweet potatoes are delicious when baked on charcoal or in the oven. They are also eaten boiled, fried or used for making puddings.

### T

**Tripe**: The lining of the stomach of a cow or goat. It is used in soups and stews.

### W

**Whip**: To beat rapidly with a hand or electric beater.

### Y

**Yam**: An underground stem or tuber. Some yams are hard in texture when cooked, and some soft. The hard ones such as yellow yam are preferably used in soups. They are boiled and served as accompaniments to meat or added to soups.

# COOKING HINTS

★ Rub ½ of a lime on your hands or cutting board to remove onion, garlic or fish odours.

★ 1 tablespoon cooking oil added to the water for boiling pasta prevents it from sticking together.

★ 1 pound coffee brews 40 cups.

★ Dip knife in hot water to slice hard boiled eggs.

★ 1 cup macaroni becomes two cups when cooked.

★ If food boils over in oven, cover with salt to prevent smoking and excessive odour.

★ Add diced, crisp bacon and a dash of nutmeg to cauliflower or cabbage for a gourmet touch.

★ To stop hinges from creaking drop a little vegetable oil on hinges.

★ Tear lettuce into pieces instead of cutting to prevent browning.

★ Cut out the core of a head of lettuce, wash the head under cold water, drain and wrap it in paper towels which have been moistened with cold water, and it will stay nice and crisp.

★ Salad dressing should not be added to salad until the last minute because the oil causes the lettuce to wilt.

★ Sour milk can be made by adding two teaspoon of lime juice to a cup of warm milk which will curdle.

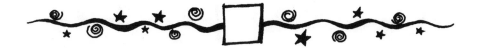

★ As soon as vegetables are tender drain and plunge into cold water. This sets the colour.

★ If too much salt has been added to soups or stews, add a potato. It will absorb the salt.

★ Fish should be kept very cold and used as soon as possible.

★ Add a little soft bread crumbs to hamburger steak to make it more tender.

★ Roasts, steaks and chops will be more tender if they are at room temperature, before they are cooked rather than taken right from the fridge.

★ A mixture of honey and mustard makes a great last minute glaze for pork or spareribs.

★ Peeling onions will cause you to shed a tear or two unless you peel them under cold running water.

★ To remove the skins from tomatoes, put them into boiling water for 1 minute — do only two at a time. Put them into the refrigerator to firm them for slicing, etc.

★ Apples and potatoes, when peeled, cored, and sliced will not turn black if immediately placed in cold salted water.

# INDEX

## A.

Ackee, in Rice and Cheese
    Casserole, 10
    with Salted Codfish,72
    with Tomatoes, 101

Appetizers, 8

Apple, Jamaican Ginger Apple
    Drink, 151

Avocado Dip, 20

## B.

Bacon, with Ackee and Salted
    Codfish, 72

Bammy, 123

Banana, Mackerel and Green
    Banana Casserole, 76
    Porridge, 142
    Baked, 145
    Daiquiri, 160
    Tropical Fruit Salad, 147

Barbeque, Jerk Pork Chops, 40
    Snapper stuffed with
    Spinach or Callaloo, 65

Beansprouts, Cabbage and Carrot
    Salad, 109

Beef, Patties, 10
    Spiced braised, 44
    with Okra, 45
    Balls, 46
    Stewed in beer, 47
    Pepper Steak –
    Jamaican-Chinese style, 49

Beverages, 149

Breadfruit, 124

Broad Beans, with Oxtail , 54

Broccoli, with Codfish , 75

Brown Cow, 161

Bulla Cake, 135

## C.

Cabbage, Corned Beef &, 83
    Curried, 103
    Rundown, 105

Callaloo, with Snapper, 65
    Salad, 77
    with Codfish, 75
    and Rice Cook-up, 102
Carrot, and Cabbage Salad, 109
    with Chicken and Sweet
    Peas, 35
    and Raisin Salad, 110
    Drink, 153

Cassava, Pudding, 133

Casserole, Ackee, Rice and
    Cheese, 104
    Ina's Mackerel and Green
    Banana, 76
    Irish Potato, 116

Chicken, Chop Suey, 50
    Curried, 34
    Fricassed, 33
    Honey Garlic Wings, 52
    Jerk Pieces, 41
    in Sweet Peas and
    Carrots, 35

Cho Cho, Macaroni and
    Vegetables, 117
    Salted Codfish &, 82

Coconut, Biscuits, 137
    Milk, 74
    Toto, 134

Codfish, with Ackee, 72
    Balls, 12
    with Broccoli, 75
    with Callaloo, 75
    Fritters, 13

Congo Peas Soup, see Gungo Peas
    Soup, 24

Corn, Bread, 139
    Cake, 132

Corned Beef, and Cabbage, 83

Cornmeal, Fritters, 92
    Turned or Coo Coo, 114
    Pudding, 130
    Porridge, 141

Cow's foot, and Lima Beans , 56

Crab, Fritters, 14
    Eggs stuffed with
    Crabmeat, 17
    Seafood spread, 18

## D.

Daiquiri, Banana, 160

Dessert, Baked Ripe Banana, 145
    Fruit Flan, 146
    Tropical Fruit Salad, 147

Doctor Fish, Fish Soup, 25

Dumplings, (Spinners), 24
    Fried, 121

## E.

Easter Buns, without Yeast, 138

Egg Nog, 157
Eggs, Stuffed with Crabmeat, 17
    with Okra, 96
    with Eggplant and
    Tomatoes, 97

Eggplant, with Scrambled Eggs and
    Tomatoes , 97
Escoveitched Fish, 60

## F.

Festival, 122

Fish, see Seafood

Fish Tea or Soup, 25

Fritters, Cornmeal, 92
  Crab, 14
  Pumpkin, 91

Fruit, Flan, 146
  Salad, 147

## G.

Ginger, and Apple Drink, 151
  Chinese Pork, 51

Gizadas, 136
Goat, Curried, 42
  Mannish Water, 26

Green Banana, Pancake, 95
  with Mackerel, 76
  Boiled, 121

Grouper, Fish Soup, 25

Gungo Peas Soup, 24

## H.

Herrings, 84

Hibiscus Flower, 154
Hominy, 143

## I.

Irish Potato Casserole, 116

Irish Moss Drink, 156

Ital, 105

## J.

Jackfish, with Spinach or
  Callaloo, 65

Jackfruit, Stewed, 118

Jamaican Coffee, 161
Jerk, Pork, 38 – 40
  Chicken, 41

Johnny Cakes, 121

## K.

Kidney Beans, Red Pea Soup, 23
  Rice and Peas, 112

King Fish, Fish Soup, 25
  Cutlets, 59
  in Coconut Milk, 66

## L.

Legumes, 111

Lentils, and Rice, 100

Lima Beans, and Tripe, 55
  and Cow's foot, 56

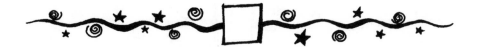

Lime, Soursop Shake &, 152

Limeade or Lemonade, 155

Lobster, Seafood Spread, 18
    Curried, 67
    Creole, 68

## M.

Macaroni, and Vegetables, 117

Mackerel, Solomon Gundy
    Spread, 16
    Rundown, 73
    and Green Banana
    Casserole, 76

Mango, Drink, 151
    Tropical Fruit Salad, 147

Mannish Water, 26

Meatballs, Cocktail, 15

## N.

Non-Alcoholic Beverages, 150

## O.

Okra, with Beef, 45
    with Eggs, 96
    Callaloo and Rice
    Cook up, 102
    Turned Cornmeal or
    Coo Coo, 114

Omelette, Spinach, 93

Oxtail, Broad Beans &, 54

## P.

Pancakes, Green Banana, 95

Papaya, Tropical Fruit Salad, 147
Pastries, 128
Patties, Beef, 10
    Vegetable, 89
Peas, and Rice, 85

Pepperpot Soup, 28

Pigeon Pea Soup, see Gungo Pea
    Soup, 24

Pina Colada, 160

Pineapple, Jamaican Salad, 108
    Planter's Punch, 159
    Tropical Fruit Salad, 147
    Pina Colada, 159

Plantain, Chips, 18
    Fried ripe, 125

Planter's Punch, 159

Pone, Cassava, 133
    Cornmeal, 130
    Sweet Potato, 129

Porridges, Banana, 142
    Cornmeal, 141

Pork, Chops on the Barbeque, 40
    Chop Suey, 50
    Chinese Gingered, 51
    Jerk, 39
    Quick Jerk, 38
Potato, Irish Potato Casserole, 116
Poultry, 31

Pudding, Cassava, 133
    Cornmeal, 130
    Sweet Potato, 129

Pumpkin, Fritters, 91
    with Rice, 99
    Soup, 30

Punch, Planter's, 159
    Rum, 159

### R.

Rabbit, Curried, 36

Raisin, Cabbage Salad &, 110
    Cornmeal Pudding, 130
    Easter Buns, 138

Red Pea Soup, 23

Red Snapper, in Brown Stew, 62
    with Spinach or Callaloo, 65

Rice, and Peas, 85, 112
    and Lentils, 100

Rum Punch, 159

Rundown, Ital style, 105
    Sauce, 73
    Shrimp, 70

### S.

Salads, Cabbage and Carrot, 109
    Carrot and Raisin, 110
    Jamaican, 108

Salted Codfish, with Cho Cho, 82
    Salad, 77
    with Seasoned Rice, 81

Sardines, 84

Seafood, 58

Seafood Spread, 18

Shad, Solomon Gundy Spread, 16

Shrimp, Chop Suey, 50
    Curried, 69
    Seafood Spread, 18
    Rundown, 70

Snapper, see Red Snapper,

Solomon Gundy Spread, 16

Sorrel , drink, 154

Soups, 22

Soursop and Lime Shake, 152

Spareribs, Pineapple, 48

Spinach, with Snapper, 65
        Omelette, 93
Spinners, 24

Sweet Potatoes, Candied, 113
        Pudding, 129

## T.

Tia Maria, Brown Cow, 161

Tie-a-Leaf, 131

Tomato, Dip, 19
        with Stewed Ackee, 101

Toto, Coconut, 134

Tripe, and Beans , 55

## V.

Vegetable, Patties, 89
        Soup, 98
        Steamed Mixed, 106

Vegetarian, 88

## W.

Watermelon, Tropical Fruit
        Salad, 147

## Y.

Yam,, Hearty Vegetable Soup, 98
        Pepperpot Soup, 28
        Red Pea Soup, 23

## Z.

Zucchini, Macaroni and
        Vegetables, 117